The Sage's Way

To
Leslie David

—

for
the utter wonder
of
passing
and
becoming

Acknowledgement for Illustrations: William Gaetz has been an accomplished vocalist, classical pianist, philosopher and photographer. But his life-long interest in the creative process and the sophisticated discipline of Zen led him to study Chinese brush painting under the tutelage of Master Professor Peng Kung Yi. He has since become a master of this technique, with works hanging in homes and businesses throughout Canada and the United States. His paintings, sold under his Chinese name Koy Sai, are still available through local galleries and from his studio in Victoria, British Columbia. *The Sage's Way* is the fifth book by Ray Grigg that William Gaetz has illustrated. In this instance, Mr. Gaetz uses the elegant and rustic simplicity of traditional Chinese brush painting to match the grounded and earthy character of *The Sage's Way*. The author deeply appreciates Mr. Gaetz's generous contribution to this book.

The Sage's Way

Teachings & Commentaries

Ray Grigg

Order this book online at www.trafford.com
or email orders@trafford.com

Most Trafford titles are also available at major online book retailers.

Print information available on the last page.

ISBN: 978-1-4120-2168-5 (sc)
ISBN: 978-1-4122-2129-0 (e)

Trafford rev. 09/20/2021

 www.trafford.com

North America & international
toll-free: 844-688-6899 (USA & Canada)
fax: 812 355 4082

Contents

The Prologue... 7
    Old Shu..8
    The Meeting... 11
    The Manuscript..22
    The Teacher...30

The Chapters...37

Acceptance	39	Learning	105
Answers	41	Losing	107
Balance	43	Man	109
Becoming	45	Mistakes	111
Beginnings	47	Mystery	113
Belonging	49	Oneness	115
Between	51	Opposites	117
Birth	54	Order	119
Body	56	Ordinary	121
Bravery	58	Patience	123
Breathing	60	Perfection	125
Changing	62	Power	127
Choosing	64	Questions	129
Compassion	66	Readiness	131
Conjoining	68	Seeing	133
Crisis	70	Self	135
Death	72	Silence	137
Doing	75	Simplicity	139
Earth	77	Solitude	141
Easiness	79	Spontaneity	143
Emptiness	81	Stillness	145
Endings	83	Strength	147
Following	85	Suchness	149
Forgetting	87	Teaching	151
Giving	89	Thinking	153
Grace	91	Trust	155
Grief	93	Uselessness	157
Heaven	95	Walking	159
Humility	97	Wandering	161
Impeccability	99	Wholeness	163
Knowing	101	Woman	165
Laughter	103	Words	167

The Epilogue...169

The Prologue

Old Shu

The same narrow path still leads from the village of Ch'ang-an in the Wu Valley, crosses a footbridge over the Han River, then wanders through a rough flatland of scattered pines and broken boulders. Beyond the fork to the Kai-tung Monastery, it begins winding upward between great outcroppings of rock, carefully searching its way to the Tien-po Temple at the base of Mount Shan. Here the path ends and the mountain towers skyward, tumbling toward the sun and moon in huge heaving masses of stone. And the people of Ch'ang-an still believe that special powers reside on this mountain because it is so close to Heaven.

High on Mount Shan, the villagers still say, grows a hidden forest of ancient trees where twisted branches breathe the clear air of wisdom and gnarled roots drink the calm of cool water. And all agree that a sage once lived in this secret place between Heaven and Earth—indeed, may even have visited their village. But no one had ever met this mysterious sage of Mount Shan. And no one had ever ventured beyond the temple to find him, for all asserted they were too busy with the affairs of ordinary life to climb such a mountain in search of such a person.

Old Shu, who was often wandering through the village and along the paths of the valley, said he had never encountered this mysterious sage of Mount Shan. Nevertheless, the villagers insisted that such a sage must exist. Who else, they reasoned, could bring the good fortune that had blessed Ch'ang-an? The seasonal rhythms of weather had welcomed both planting and harvesting, the fields of the Wu Valley had been bountiful, even the catches in the Han River had been generous. So the passing of their lives, without the famines and wars of earlier years, had assumed a natural and ordered grace. In brief, they contended, the harmony of Heaven that pervaded their village and valley was testament to the influence of a sage.

Indeed, only the presence of a sage could account for the ragged manuscript that was found beside the path near the Tien-po Temple. Although no one could agree whether the writings were old or new, no one could doubt that such a find confirmed that a sage was living among them. So, in the comfort of a confidence that arose from unquestioned conviction, the people speculated and imagined who this sage might be.

8

Once, during a gathering on a Ch'ang-an street, one man even joked that Old Shu might be this mysterious sage of Mount Shan. The other men laughed uproariously at the obvious absurdity. Old Shu himself flashed a broad grin, his eyes shining and dancing as he cocked his head sideways to look up at their mirthful faces. The mature women in the gathering just smiled with polite restraint. Other women shuffled awkwardly at the questionable humour. But the younger villagers, too unschooled in social proprieties to control themselves, giggled openly at the suggestion — a suggestion that would not have been so comical if Old Shu had not seemed so confused and forgetful, so lost and different. Or, perhaps, if he had not looked so strange.

Old Shu was a hunchback. His shoulders towered above his head, his neckbone pointed to the sky and his chin rested on his belly button. His bent and twisted body was a disordered heap of flesh and bones — ribs draped over hips, vital organs hanging upside-down, hands dangling beside his feet.

Despite this condition, he managed well enough. With eyes so close to the ground he found useful things to trade and sell. By weeding gardens and gathering firewood, he earned a few extra coins. From harvested fields, he gleaned a little grain for his winter stores. During famines, he was given extra rations of rice because the government officials thought he was crippled and helpless. When wars broke out, he was never conscripted because the passing armies considered him unfit and useless. "My twisted body has adjusted to itself," he once said, "and I have accepted its strangeness. By learning to live with myself, I have learned to live with the world. And by knowing myself, I have found more than myself."

Old Shu said many things but the villagers did not usually listen. Sometimes they found him difficult to understand because he talked about subjects that did not interest them. Sometimes he made no sense at all, as if his thinking had become as peculiar as his body. Other times he was strangely silent. Or he wandered away and no one saw him for days.

So the people of Ch'ang-an decided that Old Shu's mind was also bent and twisted, as upside-down as his organs. They listened politely when he spoke. They treated him with patience and tolerance, with the bemused respect accorded to his age and condition. But they did not take him seriously. And they did not

9

hear what he had to say. Besides, when all was well in their village and valley, when they were contented with the unfolding course of their lives, what was the need for the musings of an old hunchback?

Once, in a serious moment, some villagers asked Old Shu for his opinion about this mysterious sage of Mount Shan. "In my whole life," he said, "I've never met a sage. And I never expect to meet one."

So the people of Ch'ang-an dismissed this as another part of Old Shu's strangeness. Besides, they all agreed, he wouldn't recognize a sage if he bumped into one. He was bent so double and his eyes were so close to the ground that the only thing he could know was the place where he was standing.

The Meeting

By wandering here and there without a thoughtful purpose — by going up and down as well as over and under — Old Shu found a way to the top of Mount Shan. So the mountain and the ancient forest that grew there, like the village and the valley far below, also became his home. And he moved with a special care in this high place so the grasses, mosses and wild flowers were undisturbed by the lightness of his passing. "The best path finds itself," he said, "and the best walking leaves no footprints."

But one afternoon on his way down the mountain, Old Shu did find footprints. He had just walked through a familiar passage of faulted stone, skirted a copse of stunted pines and was approaching a high ledge for a last full view of the Wu Valley, when he noticed a patch of trampled grass. Beyond stood a young man with his back to the mountain. As still and silent as the nearby trees, he was poised precariously on a sharp edge of stone that plunged vertically to distant treetops and the shapes of broken rocks.

Old Shu moved with his usual unhurried ease to the same edge, sat down a body's distance from the young man and dangled his feet into the empty space. He waited a thoughtful moment before speaking.

"This is a very high mountain," he said in a calm and level voice that might have been a casual comment about the weather or a cursory greeting to a passing villager in Ch'ang-an.

The young man did not respond. He neither turned his head nor shifted his gaze from the abyss that fell away at his toes.

"And it's a long way down," added Old Shu matter-of-factly. Then he cocked his head sideways and looked up at the tearstained face of the young man. "Ah," he said without a traceable measure of either alarm or urgency, "the feelings of your body are at war with the thoughts of your mind."

The young man still did not respond.

"When life is ready for death" continued Old Shu, "such a difficult decision will make itself. Decisions that are too

11

early — like those that are too late — are always difficult to make. Your dilemma seems serious to you. But your troubles are everyone's troubles. And everyone dies when their lives are finished. In Ch'ang-an, even in ordinary times, someone dies nearly every day. For you to choose either life or death is an important matter. But in the wholeness of things, it's a small matter."

Then Old Shu thought for a moment and added, "Those who are alive can choose death. But no one knows if those who are dead can choose life. Perhaps that's the only important difference between life and death."

Now, Old Shu, too, was looking pensively into the abyss. Beyond its empty space, the living valley and the distant hills spread in a wonder of light and form that seemed so substantial and real. But, when he closed his eyes, the landscape disappeared and the emptiness of the abyss rushed inside to fill him with a dark mystery. When he opened his eyes, the valley and hills appeared again. How could he be certain that this transformation from nothing to something would always occur? So he closed and opened his eyes several more times. And each time the light and form became more delicate, more fragile, more tenuous. And each time the scene before him became less familiar, less understandable. And the abyss grew larger and larger until he felt it would consume him, the young man, the mountain, the valley, and everything beyond. "If I don't even understand what I see and I know," he thought, "if even certainty is uncertain, how can I understand anything?" And he became as quiet as the great stillness of Mount Shan.

Then, as if he had the eyes of the mountain, he saw an old man and a young man — one sitting, the other standing — suspended between valley and sky, balanced together on the edge of death. The soft silence of the lacy treetops reached up from far below, inviting them into the waiting time they both must travel in the body's journey back to the welcoming earth.

Just then, a hawk, following updraughts along the close curve of the cliff, sliced through the air below them, the invisible path of its whispered flight dividing the distance between what is and what will be. The cutting wings ended Old Shu's silent musings and his attention returned to the young man and their place together on the mountain.

12

"Each moment of life is like this," said Old Shu. "We are all poised on the edge of death, balanced between one mystery and another. That's why every moment is so important—because death is only an instant away. One move here, and life continues. One move there, and death comes. But if death is so close, why don't people notice? Because they're too busy with life. That's life's wisdom. Even though death is always waiting, life is too busy with itself to pay attention. Look at the two of us. Just a simple move, a long rush to the trees and rocks below, then we'd both be dead. If we don't decide to jump, maybe something else will decide for us. So what would be the difference? Death is the same whether we decide or something else decides for us. It's the same with life. So here you are trying to decide between life or death when it makes no difference at all."

"For myself," continued Old Shu after a thoughtful pause, "I'm ready for death. But each death finds its own time. So who am I to decide when it should come?"

He looked up at the young man. "And by the look of your tears, it's not for you to decide, either. To waste life with a fear of death is unwise. But life has something in it that makes people uneasy about choosing death. This uneasiness has nothing to do with the value of life—life comes and goes all the time. It's because life is bigger than each person, and we're each too small to impose our own will on its wisdom. Since we didn't chose life, we shouldn't choose death, either. Your tears are the overflowing of a life that's still full of itself. And you are trying to decide what's not yours to decide."

Old Shu again looked up at the young man, who for the first time looked back. "Besides, that's my path down there. I use it often. If you jump from here, you'll land right on top of it. The mess of guts and bones would ruin the beauty of my mountain walks." Then he smiled with a blend of levity and compassion.

During the silence that followed, the same hawk made another pass across the face of the cliff, this time from the opposite direction and a little higher, close enough that Old Shu could see the intricate, feathered patterns on the top of its outstretched wings, and the turning of its head as it searched the mountainside for prey.

"I've been visiting Mount Shan for many years," said Old Shu, "but you're the only other person I've ever seen here. How

13

did you find your way?"

"I followed you," said the young man.

"Ah," responded Old Shu. "So you know about the passage beside the old tree and under the big boulder?"

"Yes."

"It's the only way up. No one else has ever found it, although I don't know if anyone has tried. There are other hidden passages, too," said Old Shu. "The way up the mountain is very difficult to find."

"I know," said the young man. "I've been trapped here for two days. I lost sight of you. I found some water and a few berries. But I couldn't find my way up or down."

"So you thought of jumping?"

"Yes."

"And you wrestled with yourself for a long time?"

"Yes."

"Do you see this heap of a body that's me?" asked Old Shu. "Many years ago I thought about taking my own life, too. I didn't, of course, but my meeting with death was very useful."

"The monks say that we each must pass through death to properly understand life."

"Yes," said Old Shu. "But they didn't mean jumping off a mountain."

"No, I guess not," said the young man, finally stepping back from the edge of the cliff and sitting down wearily on the warm rock. Old Shu swung himself back as well, and the two sat side-by-side. With the valley spread beneath them, they looked very much like two friends who had just climbed a mountain to enjoy the view.

Shadows from the low afternoon sun now accentuated the

contours of the valley and the hills beyond. The fertile fields began to glow warmer in the soft light. And the flowing ribbon of the Han River, without the brilliance of its reflective silver, became a dark, serious line across the Wu Valley.

"I climb Mount Shan for the distance it gives me," said Old Shu. "When I'm high on the mountain, I have a sense of the world that I sometimes lose when I'm down in the valley. The valley is so full of life that it sometimes overcomes me. The mountain is life, too—but it's a special kind of life. It's also death, like the death-in-life that your monks tell you about. So I come up the mountain to die, to be cleansed, and to be born again. Whenever I need to be reborn, I come up this mountain. On the steep path, I slowly breathe out my old self. And as that little self falls away, I become empty and formless again. Then I look and I see, and I become a new Old Shu."

"So your name is Old Shu."

"That's what I'm called. But what I really am doesn't have a name. I live in the village, in the valley and on this mountain—wherever the world will have me."

"I live in Kai-tung, in the monastery," said the young man. "My name is Li Sung-chi. One of my chores is to gather firewood."

"But you didn't come up here to gather firewood," said Old Shu playfully.

"I was gathering firewood when I saw you leaving the path by the temple and decided to follow you. I don't know why. The monks in the monastery were talking about a manuscript, a sage of Mount Shan and a magical place on the mountain. I'm searching for a way in my life because I'm confused, because I can't find what I need to know. Then I got lost on this mountain, too. I couldn't go up and I couldn't go down. It's the same with my whole life," said Sung-chi. "I can't go forward and I can't go backward. So what's the use of such a life?"

"Ah," said Old Shu incisively. "If you can't go forward and you can't go backward, then you must be stopped. And that's a very useful place to be. When you're stopped, your mind penetrates deeply and you understand things you can't

15

understand at any other time. It's like death-in-life. Only when you're stopped can you move with an inner stillness. And that's the best way to move. When I get confused or lost, I stop. Then I become attentive and I wait patiently until the Great Oneness moves me. When I'm guided by something that's bigger than myself, then I always do what's appropriate. I find grace by moving inside the stillness of the Great Oneness. To do this, I become still within myself. When I move in stillness, I move with an unknowable wisdom. And then the world looks after me. If you're truly stopped, this is a very important place to be because you've found your own stillness."

Old Shu paused a moment and then asked, "What's your stillness teaching you?"

Sung-chi tried to understand what Old Shu had said. And then he searched to find a reply. But he could not find his stillness so he could not find its teaching. "I don't understand," he said. "I just feel very lost and confused."

"What's the urge that arises from deep within yourself?" asked Old Shu. "Think the thought that comes to you. Say the words that enter your voice. What you have yet to understand comes from the stillness within yourself. What do you know before you have an understanding of it?"

"Before I have an understanding of it?" repeated Sung-chi, sensing that maybe his question had just obscured the answer he might have found.

"Yes. What arises in you of itself? If you were a stream flowing down Mount Shan, what would you do and what would you say? What's flowing freely within you and through you?"

Sung-chi tried to imagine that he was a stream flowing down Mount Shan. "I'm moving but I don't know where I'm going. I feel thoughtless and empty—and clean. I'm alive and I'm not dead. But I also feel confused and lost, like I can't think and I've stopped understanding. I seem to have no past or future. And I don't know what to do next."

"Nothing is next," said Old Shu. "The stream thinks nothing about what's next. And how can you be confused and lost if you're thoughtless? Here you are—empty and clean and

16

alive — poised on the edge of the mountain of life and death. This is all you need to know. Listen inwardly. What's arising in you now? What's the next urge that comes from your stillness?"

"To tell you," said Sung-chi, "that I'm unworthy to be a monk, to be a son, and to be a man."

"Then," said Old Shu, "you must tell me — not because of me — but because this is your urge. What comes next must come of itself. When these urges are strong enough to carry you, don't resist them. When they come from the deepest place within the stillness of yourself, you'll do what you should do. Then you'll have no doubt, you'll feel no resistance. But this is too easy to be easy. And the stillness is very difficult to find. Practice is required. But for now, just follow the urges that come. Now, say what you have to say."

"It's simple," said Sung-chi. "My father wanted me to become a scholar in the imperial court of Emperor Yao. I ran away from home to become a monk. So he disowned me. Now I've fallen in love with a young woman and she occupies all my thoughts. After studying for nearly four years, I can no longer think of being a monk. During sutra readings, I think of her. In meditations, she fills my thoughts. The monks say that thoughts are like clouds, that when they come I must learn to let them go. But what am I to do when the entire sky of my mind is one endless cloud? I take a breath and she enters me. I breathe her out and then I breathe her in again. My body is full of her. She lives within me — like breathing itself. She is a voice that calls my thoughts in a way I must answer. But I have no family, no money, no land, no possessions. And I am a monk so I cannot marry her. I can only dream. Is a life of dreams worth living?"

"Life, itself, is a kind of dream," said Old Shu, "And it's also not a dream. What life do you want?"

"Once, I wanted to be a monk, so I followed the urge of my mind. But now I've awakened to something else, and I must follow the urge of my heart. My mind will not obey the orders I give to it. Now it wants to be with Mei-lin. So what am I to do?"

"Well," said Old Shu, "minds usually think too much. And a wise heart is usually wiser than a wise mind. Your mind can easily trick you, but your heart is closer to life. Like your flesh and bones and blood, your heart grows from the soil and stones and water of the Great Oneness—we are all born from the body of its wisdom, and this is the wisdom we all seek. The mind tries to follow the same wisdom as the heart, but it's so far from the ground its thoughts are easily blown here and there by the winds that come from anywhere. The body needs air for breathing, water for drinking, and a solid place for walking, so it stays connected to the wisdom of the Great Oneness. But minds can easily get lost. Thinking with just the mind forgets the body. Follow a mind and you'll invariably get lost. When this happens, ask your mind to think like an empty sky. At least an empty sky has the stillness of stone. Maybe then your mind can connect with the rest of yourself. For now, it's better to think with your body because it's closer to the wisdom of the Great Oneness."

"But," said Sung-chi, "I am thinking with my body—with my whole body. I'm restless and I'm full of urges that I can't control with my mind. My heart, my flesh, my bones—my whole body has taken over my mind."

"And so it should be," said Old Shu. "This is an important part of your journey. But you have not yet found your wholeness. You went to the monastery and you thought without feeling—and that nearly killed you. Then you met Mei-lin and you felt without thinking—and that nearly killed you. Now you must bring the two opposites of yourself together so you can be balanced and whole. Then you'll find stillness and peace."

Sung-chi listened morosely while Old Shu continued earnestly. "Your whole body is using Mei-lin to draw you into the fullness of life. This is as it should be. What would we be without our bodies? What would we be if we followed only our minds? Minds are not the wholeness of life. But let them think so, and they'll cause nothing but trouble. Minds by themselves have no sense of balance. So the mind has to think with the body, too. The top of the head has to be connected to the bottom of the feet so thoughts understand with wholeness. And then the feet have to walk on the ground so the wisdom of the Great Oneness can pass through the body and enter the mind "

"But what do I do now," asked Sung-chi, "now that I'm listening to my body?"

"First," said Old Shu, "you should thank it for not

jumping off this mountain. If you'd listened to your mind, you'd be splattered on my path. Then you need to ask your body what to do next. What does it say?"

"It says it's hungry."

" And what does it say next? Listen carefully."

"My body says it's tired from struggling with my mind. It wants a place to rest. And it says it doesn't care where it lives," said Sung-chi.

"Does it say anything else?"

"My body feels very tired," said Sung-chi. "It feels defeated. It also feels quiet—even peaceful—as if it has surrendered and died. My mind feels the same way, as if it, too, has been defeated. It doesn't know what to think or believe any more. But something is still alive inside, as if a beginning is trying to form itself but can't find a place to start. Now I'm remembering what you said about coming up the mountain to die—isn't that what you said—to die, to be cleansed and to be born again."

"Are these things telling you anything," asked Old Shu?

"That a beginning is waiting. That I should be patient."

"And what does this mean?"

"That I should go back to the monastery."

"Then," said Old Shu, "let's go down the mountain."

They walked in silence. Sung-chi followed Old Shu, the young man carefully attending to each step of the descent. Whenever he could, however, he glanced at the strange shape in front of him, marvelling at the lightness of the old man's walking. It was not so much a walking as a dancing or a playing, as if he were watching a body delighting in its contact with the various textures and contours of the mountain—each foot, step after step, meeting and touching the soil and stones with the sensual caress of a lover. Sung-chi began to think of Mei-lin again, and was glad that he was still alive.

When they reached the secret passage, Old Shu slipped beneath the boulder and Sung-chi followed him into the rich darkness of damp stone and musty soil. When they emerged into the lower opening beside the old tree, the fading light of the afternoon seemed brighter than moments before, and the air smelled fresh and clean and welcoming. In Sung-chi it generated a sense of expectation and urgency—almost exultation—and the need to stay close behind Old Shu as they eased their way down the last steep slope and into Sung-chi's familiar world.

At the base of the mountain, they passed quietly through a copse of pines beside an outcropping of stone that separated Mount Shan from the outer grounds of the Tien-po Temple. Then they reached the path to Ch'ang-an, and a little later the fork that led to the Kai-tung Monastery. This is where they stopped.

"What does your body say now?" asked Old Shu.

During the silence of their walk, Sung-chi had been attending to his body's messages and was ready for the question. "My legs are tired. My mind is more peaceful so it's recovering from its struggle with my body. My stomach is still hungry. And my heart feels like it's going home, so the monastery is where I belong for now. But I have another feeling, one that seems to be everywhere, filling the inside of me with an ache that is both a joy and a sorrow." He paused a moment before continuing.

"Shu," said Sung-chi, earnestly addressing the old hunchback with a tone of combined familiarity, respect, affection and gratitude. "I feel like you have become a part of my life, a part of my very body. I have taken you into me and now we are going separate ways. You have entered my deepest self. . . ."

But he could not finish his sentence. Finally, through rising tears, he was able to continue. "I want to study and learn from you. Will you teach me what you know?"

Sung-chi had not intended to be so abrupt with such an important request. Its implications seemed to invite more care and diplomacy. But a panic was rising in his chest and these were the only words that would release through the growing tightness in his throat. Then the wetness welling in his eyes changed the distinctive shape of the old man into a blur that melded with the shadowed stones and bushes edging the path.

Without a clear vision of Old Shu, and without the sound of his own words, Sung-chi felt that he was standing alone in the world—empty, fragile and afraid—and in that moment he suddenly felt very small, very insignificant and very vulnerable.

Old Shu's voice was gentle. "I know nothing. And I have nothing to teach. I have no beginning and no ending in myself. Without one thing or another—without differences—what would I teach? And how would I begin without a beginning?"

Then Old Shu added softly, "You seem to be a young man and I seem to be an old hunchback. But these are only appearances. We're really one and the same. So how could you have taken me into yourself? We have always been together and we will always be separate. Although you may think I saved your life, that life is neither yours nor mine to save. There is no Old Shu and there is no Sung-chi. And yet everything is as it seems. You already know what you are asking to learn. What you seek is already alive within the wholeness of yourself. There is nothing more to know than this."

Old Shu paused, waiting for these words to enter Sung-chi and for more to arise within himself.

"Your silence, Sung-chi, asks if we will meet again. I don't know what will happen until it happens. Time will find its own time. Be attentive. And be patient."

And with that, Old Shu walked alone along the path toward Ch'ang-an and disappeared around the darkening form of a great stone.

The Manuscript

The market in Ch'ang-an was a tumult of buying, selling and trading. The vendors, mostly farmers from the Wu Valley, were joined by a few enterprising householders from the village and some wandering peddlers with exotic goods from distant places. All had set up their stalls just after dawn and by mid-morning were earnestly engaged with the gathered crowds

A cacophony of haggling and negotiating, bantering and chattering, shouting and laughing competed with a background racket of banging pots and pans that some vendors were beating to attract attention to their wares. Some people took time to visit and gossip amid the din. Colorful arrays of fruits and vegetables glowed in the early sunlight. Golden carcasses of chickens and ducks, marinated and smoked to a succulent brown, hung beside open buckets of slithering eels, twitching fish and flayed snakes. Silent bolts of silk, wool and broadcloth stood near sedate sacks of rice and grains. The cool scent of the river mixed with the sweet warmth of fresh baking. Aromas of herbs and spices blended with the fragrant steam of stewing hot-pots, which wafted with the blood-smells of newly butchered animals and the drifting odours of nearby dung. From the edge of the market came the squeals of worried pigs and the bleats of anxious sheep. Restless donkeys brayed.

Old Shu moved comfortably amid this tumult. Except for a few brief words of recognition from villagers, few people acknowledged him. But he contentedly filled his senses with the vitality of the morning. And as he wandered through the crowds he caught snippets of news and gossip, fragments of conversations, portions of transactions between cautious buyers and hopeful sellers.

He himself had just traded a few sticks of dry firewood for a small bag of coarse rice when he noticed a young woman standing behind a stack of carefully piled fruits and vegetables at a farmer's stall. Actually, he realized, he became aware of her because she had been watching him. This he knew because he caught her eyes avoiding his at the moment of contact. But that moment slowed time, a pathway opened between them, and something wordless was said.

This contact was not the usual curiosity he attracted as a

hunchback. Neither was it the impersonal query that a searching vendor would give to a potential customer. He felt that she had been looking at him for some other reason— perhaps only briefly—and the intensity of this seeing left a remnant trace in the space between them, the way departing footsteps leave a dry after-image on the wet surface of hard sand. And he became aware of how much he had learned about her in the brevity of this contact.

Her eyes were bright and clear, her smooth skin tanned by work in the fields. Although soiled and weathered from this work, she seemed to glow softly with an inner light. Her bones were delicate but strong. She moved freely and lightly, with a fearless grace. She had a strength and dignity, an assurance or confidence that may have come from particular responsibilities or an unusual independence. But she was also inconspicuous, and her qualities required a special seeing to be noticed amid the earthy tumult of the market.

Old Shu realized that she was uniquely beautiful. Indeed, rather than being born, her grace suggested she could have sprouted from the living soil, arising into the world with the slow serenity of a growing flower rather than arriving with the urgent pain and rushing blood of birth. And in the fullness of this awareness, it seemed to Old Shu that she became something more than herself—like the melding of Heaven and Earth into one living form. "Ah, yes," he said to himself, "there is something special about this young woman." But he felt no need to remain where she was so he went on his way, past bamboo cages of live chickens and ducks where the roosters and drakes were still courting, with undiminished ardour, the attention of the females.

Near the end of the market morning, while Old Shu was washing his feet in the cool water of the Han River, someone came and quietly took a place beside him on the large stone where he sat.

"These are for you," a female voice said softly.

When he turned and looked up, she passed him a tied bundle of fresh persimmons. He was not surprised to see the same young woman from the market.

"You are Shu," she said evenly—a statement rather than a

23

question.

"Yes," he answered, somewhat unnecessarily. And as he measured the wealth of information embodied in her few words, he realized that this was one of those special moments which is already familiar when it happens—a special moment which belongs in no other time or place and is immediately comfortable and expectant with promise.

She waited before speaking again. Old Shu sensed that she was doing a final appraisal of him, checking to confirm to herself that the approach she had decided upon was still appropriate. But the name she used to address him, the tone in her voice, the gift, and the careful way she offered it to him—even her closeness to him on the stone—revealed what she would do. When she spoke, she spoke directly and clearly.

"Sung-chi told me about his meeting with you. He can't come to the village so he asked me to find you. My name is Mei-lin."

Old Shu let the sound of her name enter inside himself so he could feel her presence more closely. "And you have already found Sung-chi," he answered, giving slow and deliberate weight to each word.

She caught the implications of his comment and barely paused before responding. When she spoke, she looked directly at him. Her words were firm and resolved. "We have known each other long enough. I bring fruits and vegetables to the monastery. He gathers firewood and does other chores at Kai-tung. That's how we met. Now we meet whenever we can. He would like to meet you again."

As if the fullness of silence were explaining itself, as if the inevitable were fulfilling itself, something was understood that did not need to be said. So, without a decision, a decision was made. And Old Shu yielded to the welcoming rightness of the moment.

He placed the persimmons in his sack with the bag of rice, tied on his straw sandals, picked up the sack, and walked with Mei-lin toward the bridge. They did not speak as they crossed the Han River and followed the path toward Mount Shan. They met

Sung-chi near the fork to the Kai-tung Monastery where he had been gathering firewood as he waited. He looked relieved to see them.

On the sunny warmth of a nearby stone outcropping they shared the persimmons while the two young people took turns describing to Old Shu the details of their meeting, their professed love for each other, and their gratitude for his intervention on the mountain. As Old Shu marvelled at the remarkable urge that draws a man and a woman to each other, Mei-lin told of her aging father, of his difficulties with her refusal to marry suitors of his choosing, and of her growing responsibilities for the farm without the support of a mother or brothers.

Sung-chi described his increasing discomfort with the political intrigues at the monastery and his disillusionment with a teaching that filled his mind but did not reach his heart. Then he told how Mei-lin had changed his life. "So," concluded Sung-chi, "Mei-lin is bound to the farm and her father. I will stay at the monastery for now. I will gather firewood, work as required, and attend the lectures and instructions. I will meditate and learn what I can to make my way in the world. Mei-lin and I will meet when we can. But I must ask you again, Shu, to be my teacher."

Old Shu looked up, appraised the persistent earnestness in his face, and noted Mei-lin's approval. Then he looked back to the ground.

"Sung-chi, I have never been a teacher except to myself. I know nothing about teaching. I live a simple life in accordance with the wisdom of the Great Oneness. What I have learned is available to everyone who thinks and feels, who watches and sees, who listens and hears. I have no answers. I understand nothing. I'm just as confused as anyone, lost in a vast mystery that bewilders me, too. I have nothing to teach you."

"On the mountain," said Sung-chi, "in a few moments, you taught me more than I learned from the monks in nearly four years of study."

"That's because the situation demanded that you learn quickly," said Old Shu. "And you were ready to learn."

"I'm ready again," said Sung-chi.

25

"But you're not poised on the edge of an abyss," replied Old Shu.

"I am," insisted Sung-chi. "I died on Mount Shan that afternoon. And I'm no longer the person who followed you up the mountain. Now my new life has brought me to another abyss that welcomes me to another death. Mei-lin is a wonder beyond all my understanding. My whole body is eager and ready. My mind is open and welcoming. I believe I can learn from you what I need to know. My heart and my belly—even my bones—tell me this is so. You told me to listen to my body."

"I also told you that your mind can easily trick you," said Old Shu. "The power of your mind and your body has filled you with a dangerous force that can either destroy you or save you. Right now your mind has filled you with foolish hope. It has filled you with dreaming. You're still thinking with your mind and it is tricking you just as before."

"But I'm not thinking with my mind," countered Sung-chi. "I'm listening to a deeper me. I don't know what to call it. I don't insist, it does. You have already taught me this. You said that when my urge is strong enough to carry me, I must not resist. Remember? That's what you said. And since we parted, this is what I've been practicing—how to follow my inner instructions."

"It's a short time that you've been listening and practicing," Old Shu reminded him.

"You also said that time finds its own time. If this is so, then the time I've spent is of little importance. And although I've not had long to be patient, I've been very attentive."

"But," said Old Shu, "you can learn to be patient and attentive without me. Besides, as I've already told you, everything you need to know is already within you. And I have no art as a teacher. You were about to jump off a mountain, so just at that moment I knew what to say. But I wasn't the teacher. The teacher was the circumstance. I just spoke to myself. It was you who decided not to jump. You were the one who listened."

"But I want to hear more," Sung-chi said earnestly. "I want you to teach me. I want Mei-lin to learn. And I want others to learn, too."

"My teaching is too simple to teach. I have nothing to say."

"But you have already taught me."

"Sung-chi," said Old Shu with exasperation, "your reason is as persuasive as your passion. You should be in the market selling tough old stewing roosters to gullible villagers. If you sold fruits and vegetables like you argue, you could make Mei-lin's father a wealthy man. And this could also be your revenge on the monastery."

They all laughed.

"But I'm not a teacher," said Old Shu, returning to his former seriousness. "I simply follow what each moment tells me. I have neither plans nor intentions. I have no idea what to teach. Each beginning arises out of the wholeness of each moment, and each wholeness arises out of its own beginning. So where is the place to begin? Beginnings must find themselves and the wholeness of each moment must not be disturbed."

Sung-chi reached into a cloth bag and pulled out a small bundle of carefully wrapped rice paper. "Have you seen this?" he asked, handing it to Old Shu.

"What is it?" asked Old Shu.

"Some writings. The people in Ch'ang-an say it's from the mysterious sage of Mount Shan. The villagers believe there is such a person. A manuscript was found near the Tien-po Temple. Now the abbot and the monks of Kai-tung are studying it. This is a copy I made of the first few chapters. I brought them because the teachings of this mysterious sage remind me of you and the things you taught me. I think you are the author of the manuscript."

"Me!" exclaimed Old Shu with exaggerated amazement. And then he tried to assume the thoughtful pose of a meditative sage, a playfulness made silly by his theatrics and absurd by the strangeness of his body.

Sung-chi and Mei-lin laughed.

"But I can barely read or write," said Old Shu. "If the abbot and the monks are studying this manuscript, then surely it's the work of a scholar and a master, not an illiterate like me?"

"No one knows who wrote it," said Sung-chi. "It was found by a priest from the temple. He noticed a leather pouch beside the path that leads to the village. He thought at first that someone had accidentally dropped it and that it rolled under the lip of a large stone. Then he discovered tooth marks in the leather, so he decided that maybe an animal—perhaps a dog, maybe even a wolf—found it somewhere, packed it for a while, then dropped it. Fortunately, it landed in the shelter of a stone."

"So it wasn't damaged by the weather?" asked Old Shu.

"There was some damage from rain. But not very much. It's quite readable. When the priest discovered that it didn't belong to anyone at the temple, he brought it to the monastery to find the owner. No one at Kai-tung knows anything about it, either. Then the abbot and some of the monks became interested in its contents. One of my duties is to make copies for study."

"Now," added Mei-lin, "all the people of Ch'ang-an are talking about the manuscript. Some say the tooth marks are not from a dog or a wolf but from a dragon, and that the teachings have come from Heaven. This must be so, they say, because it was delivered by a dragon, saved by a stone, and then presented to a priest. They say it must contain great wisdom. And now it's the duty of the priests and monks to tell them what it means."

"Those who say it comes from Heaven," said Sung-chi, "say it's very old. And those who are skeptical say it's just some ragged pages that have been badly stored—perhaps in a hut—and handled many times by soiled hands. But the others reply, based on accounts they've heard from the priests and monks, that the graceful flow and easy freedom of the calligraphy is too masterful to be done by anyone ordinary. They argue that the purity of Heaven has combined with the soil of Earth to make the manuscript even more precious."

"And what do you think?" asked Old Shu.

Sung-chi was silent for a moment. "My mind divides wholeness into Heaven and Earth," he said. "And with the invention of purity and soil, it has created even more differences. But my inner sense tells me that the differences between one thing and another are unnatural. If this is so, then the source of the manuscript is unimportant."

"And, therefore," said Old Shu, completing Sung-chi's reasoning, "whether or not I am the author of the manuscript is also unimportant?"

While Sung-chi admired his own insight and eloquence about differences, he also had the feeling that he was being undone by his own ingenuity. And he began to regret his answer even as he gave it. "That's correct," he said slowly, after a long and reluctant pause.

"So, if you're able to see beyond me," continued Old Shu sternly, "and you're able to see beyond Heaven and Earth, then what's the need for me? And what's the need for Heaven and Earth? And without differences to separate one thing from another, what's the need for teachers and students? Now you must answer why you brought this manuscript and what it has to do with me?"

"The manuscript," said Mei-lin abruptly, "is to be the beginning of your teaching of Sung-chi."

The Teacher

Sung-chi and Mei-lin felt exposed and embarrassed by their transparent attempt to manipulate Old Shu into becoming Sung-chi's teacher. They glanced at each other and then looked awkwardly at the ground.

But, as Sung-chi had explained earlier to Mei-lin, if they tried to secure Old Shu as a teacher, they faced a dilemma. If each beginning was to have a natural easiness—as Old Shu seemed to understand was necessary—then where was the opportunity for individual volition or will? Sung-chi had not planned his misadventure on Mount Shan or his meeting with Old Shu. Yet these things had happened. And these same unintended events became the unplanned opportunity for Old Shu to teach him. But, if they wanted to learn more from Old Shu, how were more opportunities to occur if they themselves did not take the initiative to create them? How were favourable circumstances to arise inadvertently? As Sung-chi had explained to Mei-lin, initiative and inadvertence seemed to be contradictions.

Until this moment, Sung-chi had found some consolation in sharing this dilemma with Mei-lin. Now he struggled alone to find a way to placate Old Shu, fearing that their strategy had offended him and endangered a chance of receiving any more of his teaching.

Old Shu seemed displeased with their contrived efforts to create a beginning for more teaching, and they felt admonished for attempting to engineer a circumstance that did not occur out of the natural flow of uncontrolled events. But what were they to do when a beginning was not happening of itself?

Their intention had been to wait for an appropriate opportunity to introduce the manuscript to Old Shu, and then to use it as the basis for his teaching of Sung-chi. And Old Shu's adamant refusal to teach, along with his insistence that beginnings must find themselves, seemed to provide the perfect opportunity to show him the manuscript. The unfolding events had drawn them into doing exactly what they had tried to do.

Why, then, were they now feeling so awkward? Because Old Shu had caught them doing what seemed to be natural but, in fact, was not. He had exposed a contrivance which, in Sung-chi's emerging insight, seemed to be the equivalent of taking one's own life. And now, just as before on the mountain, Sung-chi felt profoundly uncomfortable, like he had attempted to do something that was in violation of some enigmatic process which he could sense but not understand. In retrospect, his ingenuity regarding the manuscript seemed superficial and silly, leaving him exposed and foolish—just as if he had tried to manipulate Mei-lin's affections by scheming and plotting. He felt unclean, as if his volition and planning had trespassed an unspoken principle that was more important than his own interests—even his own life—although no one, not even Old Shu, had ever said so. And it was of little consolation to him that he now had an accomplice in Mei-lin.

Although he and Mei-lin had used this strategy as a means of convincing Old Shu to be Sung-chi's teacher, they could find mitigating arguments to excuse their actions. They were not responsible for the discovery of the manuscript. They had not brought it to the Kai-tung Monastery or to the attention of the abbot. They had not decided that it was to be studied or that Sung-chi was to make copies of it. Indeed, they were part of a process but they were certainly not all of it—and they seemed to be responsible for very little of what was happening. So Sung-chi could not decide whether his initiative could be considered contrivance or whether it was just another part of a process that simply had a momentum and a direction which he did not understand. And nothing explained Old Shu's part in the process. Was he in control or was he just another inadvertent element in the unfolding events?

Old Shu was a mystery to Sung-chi, and who he might be had already been the subject of long discussions with Mei-lin. Was the old hunchback the author of the mysterious manuscript? This was Sung-chi's first impression. But, when the abbot assigned him the task of copying the chapters, he had just returned from the mountain to the monastery and his memory of Old Shu was still fresh and vivid—possibly exaggerated. Could this have affected his judgment? After further thought, he began to doubt this first impression—the manuscript seemed too serious, too ponderous, too scholarly to be Old Shu's. But, as thought collided with feeling, he only became more confused. Was Old Shu the mysterious sage of Mount Shan? If what he said were true—that he came to the mountain often but had never met anyone there until Sung-chi's impetuous arrival—then perhaps he was the elusive sage. But maybe there was no sage. What, then, would explain the presence of the manuscript?

Even more baffling for Sung-chi, however, were the events that brought together the manuscript, Old Shu and himself. Was something more than mere chance moving these events? Sung-chi could not decide whether some person or force was steering all the parts in a predetermined direction, or whether all these connections were just coincidental. Consequently, he could not decide whether he and Mei-lin were active initiators of their own behaviour or just players who were being carried along in a larger order that had a will of its own. It also dawned on Sung-chi that maybe he was asking questions that need not be asked—thinking the wrong way—and that the entire dilemma was of his own making. The more he thought, the more uncertain and confused he became.

The new information he had gathered in the last few minutes also crowded into his thoughts. Old Shu had not denied authoring the manuscript. But he also had said he could barely read or write. However, as before with Old Shu, Sung-chi had some difficulty determining what was serious and what was playful—the old man seemed to treat play seriously and to treat seriousness playfully.

Meanwhile, Old Shu had apparently returned to his usual calm, and seemed to be accepting the present circumstances with his customary easiness. He was now responding to his conscription as Sung-chi's teacher with apparent equanimity—at least, as well as Sung-chi and Mei-lin could determine, the sternness had disappeared.

"When the rain falls," said Old Shu to himself, but loud enough for the two conspirators to hear, "it falls freely. And when the sun shines, it shines without effort ."

Sung-chi glanced at Mei-lin for some hint of what Old Shu meant. Was it exasperation or acquiescence? Her quizzical expression did not help. So, because of an uncertain reading of Old Shu's mood and the lesson learned from the blatant failure of their manuscript strategy, Sung-chi decided to be honest and direct.

"It's true," said Sung-chi, "that Mei-lin and I have been talking. I told her about my despair, about our meeting on the mountain, and about my desire to be taught by you. Everyone in the village and the valley knows that you go your own way, that you have your own way of doing things — that's not quite what they say, but that's what they mean. So we knew we would have difficulty finding a path to follow with you." He paused before continuing.

"If we were to find a way for you to teach me, we had to find a beginning because — as I remembered — you said that you could not find a beginning in yourself. Without such a beginning, how could you start to teach me? And yet you did. On the mountain, the beginning found itself. So you taught when you did not intend to teach and I learned when I did not intend to learn. As you said, it seems that life does not belong to us. If this is so, then we are contained in something greater than ourselves. And, whatever Mei-lin and I may do, it cannot trespass or offend you. If we cannot understand our deepest selves because they are the hidden answer beyond all our searching, then the same is true for Mei-lin and me. And in such an answer there is no answer — only what is."

Sung-chi paused for a long moment, somewhat surprised by what he had actually said. Old Shu waited patiently. Mei-lin was anxious, concerned that Sung-chi had said something foolish, or had said nothing at all, or — worse still — had offended Old Shu.

Then Sung-chi took a deep breath. It was a spontaneous gesture made by a mind and body that felt they needed to fill before they could empty of the thoughts and feelings which were inside. When he continued, he felt a strange transformation — that in his deepest centre he was no longer trying to convince Old Shu to be his teacher. Nor was he trying to justify his manipulative strategy of attempting to create a beginning for Old Shu's teaching. He was simply speaking, almost without thought and to no one in particular. His voice, no longer insistent, had become soft and level, relaxed and sure. It conveyed a peacefulness as if he, Sung-chi, were no longer asking, no longer needing — as if his voice did not even belong to him.

"Without differences," he said directly to Old Shu, "there is not a separate you or me. There is no teacher or student, no life to save or lose. Nothing is owed. There is no start or finish, no beginning or ending. Because of this, you will be able to teach without teaching and I will be able to learn without learning. This is what you and the mountain have already taught me."

Old Shu smiled at the stillness in Sung-chi, waiting in silence for the promise of more words.

Sung-chi continued. "A manuscript came, but where it came from no one knows. Maybe it was delivered from Heaven by a dragon. Maybe it was stolen from a hut by dogs. None of this matters. What is here is simply here. Because of mind and body, because of thoughts and desires—because of all things together as one—the three of us are here. We have been joined together by the circumstances of ourselves and by all other things—by the wisdom, as you would say, Shu, of the Great Oneness."

When enough silence had passed to confirm that Sung-chi was finished, Old Shu spoke.

"Sung-chi, you have already learned many important things from the Kai-tung Monastery. What you have said is rich with more than I have taught you. But the mountain, as you have said, has also taught you. And you are beginning to hear the wisdom that lives within yourself.

"I'm a simple man who has never had a student. And I know nothing about teaching. But you have found a way to convince me to be your teacher. You have used your own devices. But these things, you will discover, are not necessary. What is important, for now, is that you have found a way to convince me. You have demonstrated determination and a measure of attention, resolve and discipline. But there is another way, one which moves with the ease and grace of water, one which requires no volition or willfulness—not even self.

"And what is this way? It's the way that brought you and Mei-lin together, the way that brought you to the mountain. It's the way that finds itself, and moves everything within an order that's greater than knowing can know.

"Your willfulness and your determination, Sung-chi, are just a beginning. And they are full of foolishness and danger. The

34

art of moving in accord with the Great Oneness will take much skill and sensitivity. But you have already learned the most important thing—that life is greater than any understanding of it. Because of this, the monastery's teachings could not capture the whole of you. It took the mountain to do that—and Mei-lin." Then Old Shu turned to her.

"Mei-lin, you are the living wisdom of the Great Oneness, the life of all things that grow from the generosity of soil and water. As a woman, you know in your bones what a man can spend a lifetime seeking. You are the birth and death of all things, the secret darkness that answers its own deepest questions. Sung-chi will find the wholeness of life through you. And you will find more than your own life through him. Together you are a wonder that is greater than any thought can think."

Old Shu waited for more words to gather into himself. Then he spoke to them both.

"I will teach the little I know so that you may learn to live this wonder in harmony and grace. We will use the mysterious manuscript as a beginning. Who knows what it will say or where it will lead us? We will meet when we meet—when the time is ready. And you, Sung-chi, may write what you wish and record what you will."

And so Old Shu left them by the path and went alone to the mountain. And the fullness within himself overflowed as tears.

The Chapters

The Teachings of the Mysterious Sage of Mount Shan
together
with
The Commentaries of Old Shu

—

As Best Remembered and Recorded
by
Li Sung-chi

Acceptance

The Teaching:

The stillness between all invented opposites is the source of acceptance and the beginning of an easiness that allows opportunity to arise from adversity. In this wordless place between struggle and submission, between strength and weakness, between certainty and doubt, acceptance is not defeat and yielding is not surrender. Here, the unfolding wholeness opens to a nameless grace. Stillness is attained when wholeness is accepted. Acceptance becomes grace when wholeness is entered. And when the wholeness of each passing moment is welcomed, the unfolding grace cannot be avoided.

The Commentary:

"I'm a hunchback," said Old Shu, "and for a long time I struggled against the burden of my deformity. Finally, I gave up struggling and I wanted to die. That's when I felt distant from my body and from myself, as if I were someone else looking at Old Shu from afar.

"But how could I not be myself, I thought? How could I not be this hunched back and these upside-down organs? Yet, there I was, looking at someone who used to be me.

"Suddenly, when I was no longer me, I felt relieved, unburdened, and peaceful—as if by losing myself, I found something of much greater value. Then, for the first time, I could see myself clearly. That's when I realized I'd never been able to see Old Shu as he really was because I'd been trying to see him as if he were someone straight and tall.

"The Old Shu who was standing before me was bent and crooked. But he was living and breathing. He could eat and drink, walk and talk. Except for his shape, he looked healthy enough. His body was a spectacle but his mind was sharp. He was shrewd and quick-witted. He may have been at war with his

39

body but he was at peace with the world. He had no enemies. He had enough to eat. By wandering aimlessly — by following inner directions — he moved in harmony with the circumstances around him and went where he belonged. By forgetting what he wasn't and being what he was, the world seemed to receive him with ease and grace. Although he looked like a strange thing, he was a walking wonder.

"That's when I realized that limitations are overcome when they're recognized and accepted. Only then can they be mastered and used. When disadvantage is understood and embraced, it becomes a source of insight and strength. Then misfortune opens to opportunity.

"With my new seeing, I saw that denial is useless and struggle is futile. And when denying and struggling are finally exhausted, then acceptance is able to find itself and become an inner stillness. With this inner stillness, I could find my proper place in the wholeness of things.

"And what's the wholeness of things? It's whatever is, whatever is seen without the blindness of self. Without a self, I became something more than myself.

"And what's an inner stillness? It's doing without having a mindful purpose. Without a mindful purpose, I became something more than purpose. When my acceptance entered the wholeness of things, I became one with the Great Oneness. And Old Shu was no longer important.

"People think I'm broken and foolish. But let them think what they like. I know otherwise. They see only the outer me, and think that this is who I am."

Answers

The Teaching:

Thoughts attempt with answers to explain the unexplainable, to limit the unlimited, to stop the endless unfolding of everything's becoming. But the boundless cannot be contained by answers, and the abiding mystery cannot be dispelled by the illusion of certainty. Because the shape of answers cannot capture the living presence of everything's becoming, knowing is always formless. Without questions, what is the need for answers? Without answers, where is the end of knowing? When something greater than answers recognizes what has always been known, then everything is the same yet different. The ordinary becomes extraordinary and insight reaches beyond answers. Answers that are finally answers have no questions — so simple that only silence can explain.

The Commentary:

"Sometimes," said Old Shu, "I walk in circles to remind myself of the foolishness of answers. People see me and think I'm strange, that my mind has become as peculiar as my misshapen body. Then they quietly pass by, pretending not to notice me. If they had stopped to ask, I would have explained what I was doing.

"When I make the mistake of asking a question, I get an answer. And when I get an answer, I get confused.

"Why do answers confuse me? Because they just create more questions, more answers and then more questions. And thoughts, chasing themselves round and round in an endless trap of their own making, are a waste of valuable thoughts. So I walk in circles to remind myself not to ask questions, not to look for answers.

"When I look out and when I look in — wherever I look — all I see is everything's changing. And answers try to stop what's forever moving and becoming. How am I to practice my own simple wisdom if I'm burdened with the confusion of answers? When I'm confined by answers, how can I wander freely within the wholeness of the Great Oneness?

"So, what do I do? I don't ask questions and I don't look for answers. I just forget and I empty until I don't even know who I am. Then I become serenely lost and profoundly confused, moving aimlessly wherever the Great Oneness takes me, carried peacefully in the grace of a vast mystery.

"Then, wordlessly and thoughtlessly, I wander the wild hills and valleys, lost in the utter wonder of being. Soaring birds fly their feathered magic through invisible air. Bending grasses dance in rustling concert with whispering winds. Ancient trees sing their unheard music to listening skies. For eyes that hear and ears that see, the silent mountains shout their distant presence. And without a single word, the secret is explained."

Balance

The Teaching:

Balance is an elusive stillness that waits in a hidden place within everything's becoming. Forever present in the nameless centre of all changing, it is an unshakable calm that is never unsettled by surprise or hurried by urgency. Always silent and unmoving, it changes but remains the same as all things rise and fall in their endless unfolding. Because it moves but is forever still, it is forever present yet undisturbed. So from the very beginning to the very end, it is a readiness that is always ready.

The Commentary:

"Strange," said Old Shu, "but every time I think I understand, I feel like I don't. And whenever I think I know, my thoughts become small and foolish, like I've lost something big and important. Then my belly gets tight, my legs become stiff, and I stumble instead of gliding smoothly through the world.

"I don't know what to call this thing I lose. It's a mystery, a something that's like a nothing or a nothing that's like a something. Whatever it is or isn't, it seems to be a freedom that allows me to move in accord with everything's changing, an easiness that keeps me within the grace of a wholeness that's greater than I can understand. Whenever I have it, I feel calm and fulfilled, in harmony with the Great Oneness.

"In this grace, there's a readiness to all I do, as if my belonging is always finding a new place for itself in a vast and unfolding order. Although I can't change this order and I can't stop its moving, it carries me with a wisdom I can trust.

"I can't describe this order because it escapes between all the words I know. And I can't explain it because it's more than my thoughts can think. But it seems to be a shapeless shape that's always moving, always changing yet always the same. Its sameness is the Great Oneness being itself. Its moving is the Great

Oneness becoming itself.

"Because I can never understand the Great Oneness and I can never know all its changing, my not-knowing leaves me free to respond without hesitation or restraint. So I don't try to understand. I don't even think. I just trust the wisdom in each unfolding moment, release to its moving, and let my doing do itself.

"The less I know and the less I expect, the more I'm able to stay in balance on the edge of everything's becoming. Without my own opinions and ideas to interfere, something bigger than myself guides me. Then I move with a readiness and a grace that leaves me easy and peaceful within the Great Oneness. I enter the harmony and the wisdom of its order. And then no matter what happens, my centre is undisturbed and I'm quiet and serene — even in the face of death."

Becoming

The Teaching:

Deep inside the silent centre of each person's becoming is a sound within a sound, a simple calling that can be heard only by inward listening. Hear the one clear call that was born before birth and lives to the very edge of death, the single voice that wordlessly whispers the secret direction. Listen more deeply than thoughts can think. Within the silence of this listening, a stillness knows the grace of each moment's becoming. When all moments are suspended in timeless quiet, then the wisdom of all change is apparent. Wisdom is order finding itself. Grace is becoming fulfilling itself.

The Commentary:

"Because I can't know who I am," said Old Shu, "and I can't know what I'll become, I let go and I follow the urges that arise from deep within myself. From my emptiness, I fill with the wonder of being. From my stillness, I overflow with the magic of becoming. From my trust, I move with the wisdom of the Great Oneness.

"How do I move with this wisdom? I stay attentive and alert. I trust everything that happens. And when I'm open and receptive, I release. Then a wholeness enters and fills me. Each moment floods me with its own fullness. I'm lifted by the grace of a thoughtless becoming, I'm carried on the blessing of a wordless wisdom, and I move in harmony with all that is.

"I'm soft and yielding yet I'm disciplined and resolute. I'm aimless and free yet I'm confined and bound. Within the bonds of a nameless order, I choose yet I don't choose, I know yet I don't know, I understand yet I can't explain, I have words yet I'm overcome by silence.

"Without a will, I'm guided by the urges in my belly and my bones, by an inner sense that my thoughts can't understand. I don't argue with myself. I don't try to justify or explain what I do. I change on impulse, without hesitation or deliberation. I move like water moves. And like a stream flowing down a mountain, I go where the beauty leads me.

"Maybe this sounds strange. Maybe no one understands what I'm trying to say. Even I don't know. How can I know what I don't know? How can I trust what confuses me? How can I follow what I can't explain? I'm always bewildered and lost, just wandering alone in a vast mystery, overcome by everything that happens. And yet I'm peacefully still. I wait yet I don't wait. I listen inwardly and I hear what can't be heard. I'm always ready. Then I move without instructions, following a silent and familiar voice that I don't even understand.

"I listen to the Great Oneness and I move in accord with its wholeness. I empty of myself and I fill with a wonderful ease. Then, in my joy and in my sorrow, in my laughter and in my tears, I enter a becoming that always takes me where I belong."

Beginnings

The Teaching:

Every beginning has a shape and a form, and its own place in the unfolding order of wholeness. Beginnings that are met with balance move in harmony with this order, gently fulfilling themselves from moment to moment. Each moment met with balance is an opportunity opened. Wise choices are beginnings made in the stillness of balance. Use this stillness to follow beginnings, and their place in the wholeness of things will be apparent. Then even the most winding and treacherous path can be travelled safely, and each new beginning opens to a nameless grace.

The Commentary:

"This is nonsense," said Old Shu. "Who would be foolish enough to separate beginnings from endings, and endings from beginnings, as if they were different?

"Within the Great Oneness, everything moves and changes endlessly. Beginnings become endings and endings become beginnings. But who knows when one becomes the other? In the wonder of wholeness, they seem to be the same to me. So I pay no attention to them.

"I take to my dragon wings a thousand times a day and I fly to the tops of mountains where beginnings and endings meet. With a body as light as clouds and a mind as empty as sky, I go where my inner urges move me. I don't care about starting or stopping. I begin when I start, and I end when I stop. That's good enough for me.

"Because I move easily in the world—because I don't disturb it with willful struggle—I notice a form in everything that happens. I don't know what to call this form and I don't know what it means. It's like a shapeless shape, like a hidden order that's more than I can understand. So I'm always lost, always

47

confused. But that seems to be the way I find myself, the way I follow the wisdom of the Great Oneness. I am but I don't know who I am. I choose but I don't know why I choose. Whenever I start, I don't know when I'll stop. And wherever I begin, I don't know where I'll end.

"Because I'm uncertain and confused, I seem to find meaning in whatever happens. Every moment seems to be a beginning that carries me somewhere important, that moves me where I belong in the unfolding wholeness. I don't understand what this wholeness is but it takes me where I feel peaceful and complete, as if I'm always doing what I'm supposed to be doing.

"Sometimes I say to myself, 'Shu, what do you know?' And I can't think of anything. So I just laugh. And then I ask myself, 'Shu, are you lost?' And I always answer, 'Here I am!' Then I laugh some more. After all these years, I must know something and I must be somewhere. Unless, of course, I'm always beginning."

Belonging

The Teaching:

Before the first question can be asked, before the first doubt can be raised—even before the first thought can be thought—the first knowing remembers the unbroken wholeness in which each thing belongs. And each thing, deep in itself, remembers this belonging. Belonging is the deep remembering that affirms the togetherness of all things. So, in quiet moments of deep listening, hear the trusted whisper of belonging.

The Commentary:

"To find my belonging," said Old Shu, "I try to find where I don't belong. So I separate myself from everything. I close my eyes and shut out the light so I'm not part of the day. I sit on a rock and lift my feet so I'm not part of the mountain. I hold my breath and pinch my nose so I'm not part of the sky. I stand sideways and pull in my belly so I make no shadow. I clap my hands and wave my arms so I'm not the silent stillness of stones. When I feel the foolishness of what I'm trying to do, I smile. And then I ask myself, 'How can I not belong?'

"At first, before I could think, I belonged. But I didn't know I belonged. Then I began to think, and I thought there was me and everything else. That's how I lost the belonging I didn't know I had. And then I struggled for a long time to find a place for myself in everything that wasn't me.

"Finally, I decided, I should return to my beginning and think again. That's when I discovered I couldn't find my belonging because I was separated from it by the me that wanted to belong. So I decided to forget myself. And as I began to forget myself, I began to find my belonging. 'Strange,' I thought, 'that I should lose my belonging by finding myself, and find my belonging by losing myself.'

"When I forgot myself, I became quiet and still in the

place that used to be me. Then the differences between inside and outside fell away. Without an inside or an outside, I became empty and open rather than full and closed. Then separateness disappeared and all my senses flooded with the wonders of the world. My seeing and hearing were fresh and alive, brilliant and clear, like I was seeing and hearing for the first time.

"Now, everything's the same again—yet different. The nearby stones breathe silently with my breathing. I inhale and hold the sky tenderly within a body that's no longer mine. I walk aimlessly on the mountain and it rises and falls beneath the passing of my selfless steps. And all the stones of the mountain and all the air of the sky sing within the place that used to be me. The world and I have become each other—an undivided wholeness thoughtlessly being itself. Does it matter if I'm Old Shu or not?

"Since I can't escape belonging, I'll just stay where I am, be what I become, and live my life contentedly. What else can I do when I'm where I belong and there's nowhere else to go? And this is how I'll die, too. When not even the winds of Heaven can blow the dust of my bones from the embrace of the Great Oneness, then even in death I'll keep my belonging."

Between

The Teaching:

A special knowing resides between the differences that thoughts have invented. Not this and not that, not here and not there, not one and not other, but in the boundless place between all distinctions. Something other than thoughts knows what thoughts cannot think. Something fills the emptiness between things and connects all differences to each other. Something says what cannot be said, hears what cannot be heard, thinks what cannot be thought, knows what cannot be known. To find what cannot be found, enter the place between everything that can be found.

The Commentary:

"From high on Mount Shan," said Old Shu, "my eyes look down on the gentle morning mists that hide the Wu Valley. My voice sounds strong and crisp in the cool air, and my thoughts seem bright and clear in this special place.

"Now I want to say something I may not be able to say, and I want to think something I may not be able to think. Maybe I can say it or maybe I can't. And even if I can say it, maybe it won't make any sense.
Nevertheless, I'm going to try.

"If a stone is just a stone and a tree is just a tree, if each is just a separate thing, then what connects them together? How do trees become forests? How do stones become mountains? How does dew and mist and rain, and even the melting snows of spring, become the streams and rivers that flow to the sea? If each dewdrop becomes part of the sea, then something must be between the parts to connect them into a wholeness that's greater than themselves.

"I don't understand this something that's between things, this something that makes all the separate things of Heaven and

Earth into more than their parts. I don't know what it is and I don't have a word for it.

"If I could say what it is, I would say it. If I could think what it is, I would think it. Whatever it is, it's not an ordinary word and it's not an ordinary thought because it seems to be in the emptiness between everything I can say and think.

"Although I can't say what it is, I can feel it in the smallness of my words, in the silence between everything I say. Although I can't think what it is, something in my ordinary thoughts seems thin and hollow as if there's something important I'm not thinking. And I can feel it in thinking's endless questions, in thinking's doubt about itself, in the uneasy thought that thinking has no end — no last thought that finally understands everything.

"Now, isn't this strange and wonderful. It's early in the morning and I'm sitting on a high mountain, playing with words and thinking about thinking. And I'm saying there's something between words I can't say. And I'm thinking there's something between thoughts I can't think. And while I'm talking about what I can't say and I'm thinking about what I can't think, the morning sun is warming the sleepy mists below me. And as they awaken and stir in the deep hold of the valley, they rise up the face of the mountain, swirling around me on their way to Heaven. The sky above is bright and clear, cloudless and empty, and the floating mists disappear into its endless blue. And somehow — I don't know how — I'm full of this fullness. I see but I don't understand my seeing. I think but I don't understand my thinking. And the beauty of what I see overflows my eyes and fills them with tears of wordless wonder.

"I see, and I feel, and I think. But I don't understand. So, without a word or a thought, I accept the wonder that holds me. Then, like mist melting into endless sky, I silently disappear into the vastness of a deep wonder. I lose myself and I lose my thoughts. And without a self or a thought, I pass between all differences, and become the grace that connects everything to everything else.

"Does this sound like nonsense? Does it make any sense? Am I saying anything at all? I'm trying to say that between differences there's something without differences, something that

52

makes the separate parts of wholeness whole. Between each thing there's something incredibly important that's too small to find and too large to think—something that can't be said or thought. Between words there's something wordless that can't be heard with ordinary hearing, and between thoughts there's something thoughtless that can't be understood with ordinary thinking.

"So, I attend to what's ordinary but I also attend to what's not ordinary. I think but I don't think. I know but I don't know. And this opens to a special kind of thinking and knowing. When the silence within me is not silent and the emptiness within me is not empty, then I enter the nameless place between all differences and I become one with the Great Oneness."

Birth

The Teaching:

Each new moment is a birth and a forgetting. The past disappears into the fullness of the present, the old becomes the wonder of the new, and each moment arrives as an endless beginning. Answers are forgotten. And without the burden of certainty, the fullness of the present arrives with unsurpassed clarity. Readiness is always ready. And each new moment is met with such simplicity that even death is as welcome as birth.

The Commentary:

"I don't remember when I was born," said Old Shu, "so I don't know how old I am. And I never count years and I don't remember yesterday, so maybe today is the beginning of my life.

"I wander from place to place, and all things are new and alive to me. The trees and grasses, the river and clouds, even the blue of the sky—everything I see is vital and shimmering with a living vibrance. The sounds of streams and birds, of wind and rain—I'm always amazed to be hearing them. The dew that comes so gently in the cool of the night blesses the mountain mosses and wets my feet during morning walks. And the fragrance of wild flowers, awakened by the rising sun, wafts from the sides of familiar paths I've never before travelled. Maybe I die each night and each morning I'm born afresh into the fullness of this most amazing wholeness.

"Maybe I die each moment, and then I'm born again in the next. Maybe that's why everything's so new and alive to me.

"Yesterday is passed and tomorrow has not yet come. So I'm just wherever I am, filled with an awareness that I can't understand. I remember but I don't remember, as if I've always been where I just arrived—as if I'm always being born and I'm always discovering for the first time. Like a child lost in wonder, I'm too enchanted even to be afraid.

"My senses flood with countless riches. Everything churns and swirls around me. But I don't understand what's happening. I just accept and trust with the purity of a newborn child. And as each moment arises, I respond with a thoughtless urge. If I think, then I become confused and lost. So I just stay wherever I am, born into the moment that holds me, somehow carried in the grace of a peaceful innocence."

Body

The Teaching:

Since the body does not speak with words or explain with thoughts, thoughts that hear with words are not listening to the body's deepest knowing. When words are silent and thoughts are still, the body will teach what it knows. So be at peace with the changing body. Move in balance with its quiet needs. Honour the sensuous desire of its flesh. Believe the rushing urgency of its blood. Trust the waiting patience of its bones. Then be both moved and unmoved, both attentive and thoughtless, both ready and receptive to another kind of wisdom.

The Commentary:

"Who am I to interfere with my body," said Old Shu. "It has a mind of its own. It has its own needs. So I let it be itself.

"How do I let it be itself? By trusting its wisdom and following its urges. When it's thirsty, I drink. When it's hungry, I eat. When it's tired, I rest. When it's sleepy, I sleep. It knows what to do. And when it's contented, it looks after me.

"So we have an understanding. I respect it and it respects me. I tell it what I want and it tells me what it wants. I work for it and it works for me. We're the burden and the blessing of each other, just one person pretending to have different parts .

"Because we're one person, we find a way to be together. When I tend to my body's needs, it leaves my thoughts free to think what they like. With my thoughts occupied with themselves, my body is free to do what it likes. When I don't meddle, it walks without stumbling, stands without wobbling, sits without fidgeting. When I don't even know how it lifts a little finger, how am I supposed to supervise all its parts, all its organs, all its cleaning and repairing? It knows how to beat its own heart, how to breathe its own breathing and take its own steps.

"I just go where my feet go. I follow them because they're always just where they are. Step by step they take me to whatever happens next. So I follow my feet and honour the urges in my belly. When I don't interfere, my body stays in balance with itself, with me and with the Great Oneness.

"My body and my thoughts seem to be different but they're really one wholeness. When the separate parts attend to each other, their differences slowly disappear and they become something special — a simple easiness that moves gracefully with itself, and then harmoniously with everything else's moving. But I can't explain how this happens.

"Without differences, who decides to stop or go, to stand or sit, to eat or sleep? From moment to unfolding moment, things just happen. I'm aware but I don't interfere. But whenever I make an effort or I try to decide, I disturb an unspoken understanding and I lose this wholeness, this easiness and this grace. Then whatever I do becomes contrived and forced, and I feel lost and confused, no longer in harmony with the Great Oneness.

"What has my body taught me? Not to struggle against it, not to resist its wisdom, not to do what it doesn't want to do. So, whatever we do, we do together.

"Someday, of course, my body will go out of balance with itself, and die. And then I'll peacefully follow it— wherever it goes."

Bravery

The Teaching:

Bravery is inner strength meeting the adversity of each unfolding moment. Because no one can know what will come and what will pass away, each new moment arrives as an unknown, surprising even itself. When one thing can suddenly become another, who knows when joy will become sorrow, when laughter will become tears, when celebration will become mourning? Enough can easily become too little and something can easily become nothing. Only an instant separates gaining from losing, success from failure, pleasure from pain, and safety from danger. Therefore, bravery must always be ready so that adversity does not become disaster.

The Commentary:

"I awake in the morning," said Old Shu. "I get out of my straw bed and I light my fire. Then I eat my rice and drink my tea. But the cool freshness of each welcoming day also offers trouble and danger.

"The countryside stirs around me as ordinary people rise to their daily affairs. Farmers, burdened with the weight of scythes and hoes, trudge to their fields of unsure harvests. Woodcutters, wielding the sharpness of axes, begin their endless labour of cutting and hewing. Shopkeepers and merchants chance another day of business. Street vendors, setting out their meagre goods, summon the selling skills that may fend off another day of hunger. Everyone—old and young—meets disease and promised death. The sick and the weary shuffle to apothecaries and doctors for a few more hours of hope. Midwives visit labouring women who are full with the implanted seed of their men. Mothers faithfully nurture growing children. Students wager their futures on the merits of study and discipline. How can anyone say these ordinary lives are easy or certain? And somewhere unknown to me— far from Ch'ang-an—others are surviving a drought, a flood or a famine. Isn't this enough

58

bravery?

"Wang-chin was a skilled swordsman who could kill a hundred men during each day of battle. Everyone called him a hero and thought he was brave because he fought in wars, destroyed armies, and received honours and favours from Emperor Yao. But his bravery is no greater than the woman who suffers the pains of childbirth, the hungry man who struggles to feed his poor family, the old and the frail who calmly meet the withering decay of age. What would happen to Emperor Yao's kingdom if no one had such ordinary bravery?

"So I honour ordinary people and the everyday things they do. No one needs to go to war to be a hero. Heroic deeds are also done by simple folk who are too busy with the burdens of life to notice their own bravery. So their bravery is even greater than a hero's bravery, and they deserve honour above honour."

Breathing

The Teaching:

In the stillness between breaths, all differences wait in silent balance. This is the timeless place where comings and goings no longer occur, where endings rest and beginnings are nourished, where something extraordinary waits to be found. But those who would know the extraordinary, who would set it apart and keep it as something separate, will lose it. For the stillness between breaths can only be kept by accepting ordinary breathing, by trusting the changing that pervades all things. Those who want the extraordinary without the ordinary will find neither. But those who seek the extraordinary within the ordinary, will find it everywhere.

The Commentary:

"Breathing does itself," said Old Shu, "so why should I bother tending to it? When I'm sitting quietly, I breathe slowly. When I'm climbing Mount Shan, I breathe quickly. I don't decide how to breathe. My body does that for me. Because I let breathing do itself, I don't interfere with its rhythm. Whether long or short, whether deep or shallow, it comes and goes as it pleases.

"I leave other things to themselves, too. My heart beats, then rests and beats again. My body sleeps, then awakens and sleeps again. I walk, I rest and then I walk again. All things come and go in the rhythm of their own breathing. When I honour the wisdom of this breathing, then I don't interfere with the comings and goings of the Great Oneness.

"During breathing, there's a still moment between each breath when nothing moves. Breathing stops—as if it were tempting death a thousand times a day. What if breathing forgot to breathe again? And what reminds breathing to breathe?

"Something stops what's moving and then moves what's stopped. Something mysterious—as still as emptiness—decides

60

to change itself. Like a mystery that's waiting between all the apparent opposites and differences of everything, it seems to make things happen. But I don't know how.

"And I don't know what to call it. It's an unknowable something that's like nothing, a vast and silent stillness that comes from nowhere and everywhere, that moves secretly through everything. And I don't know what it is. But I can feel it in my own stillness, in the place between my thoughts, and within all the things I do.

"It breathes me in and out, and it touches me with peace and serenity. When I trust it and I let go, its stillness becomes my deepest balance. And with this balance, I move easily with everything that moves — like breathing breathes itself."

Changing

The Teaching:

All the countless parts of wholeness arise and appear, then change and reappear in different forms. Everything changes—except the changing itself. To find the place where changing does not change, enter the changing. Trust and release into the becoming and passing of all things. Do not resist. Empty of self, of desires and of all certainty. When the changing is entered, differences disappear, movement stops, and changing no longer changes. In this stillness, greatness is hollow, fame is vanity, and all treasures are as nothing. Then wholeness will be apparent and all changing will be calmly accepted.

The Commentary:

"Everything changes," said Old Shu. "And I change, too. But my changing is different.

"What's the difference? Most people resist changing because they think it causes trouble. Maybe they're afraid of the unpredictable or maybe they don't want to lose control. But they don't seem to recognize that changing is the unfolding order of the Great Oneness.

"Following this order requires discipline. And without discipline, people get lost and confused. When they think too small, when their vision is too narrow and too self-interested, they get distracted and upset with all the little things that happen. If they had the discipline to think big enough, they'd be able to think small enough, too, and moment by moment they'd follow the order that moves in all changing.

"This order isn't always easy to follow. Sometimes it leads me gently from place to place. Sometimes it grabs me by my neckbone and heaves me from here to there. Then I land in a heap, pick myself up and ask, 'Who am I to complain when the Great Oneness moves me according to its wisdom? What's it teaching me? What am I supposed to be learning?' That's what I mean by discipline. Regardless of what happens, I keep my centre and I keep my balance. That's what's needed to follow the order that moves in all changing.

"I didn't notice this order when I was young because I was too busy doing what I wanted, too busy struggling against the circumstances that blocked my way. Then I slowly began to realize I was moving and changing according to an order that was bigger than myself. So I learned to recognize this order, to accept everything's changing and to follow the wisdom of the Great Oneness.

"This requires a special discipline. First I have to know who I am — not the outer me who people recognize, not even the inner me who thinks and feels, but the me who remains the same from birth to death. This is my centre, my balance, my selfless place in the Great Oneness. When everything's changing, I need the discipline to keep what doesn't change.

"Therefore, I let the changing change but I keep what's deepest, what's still and silent, what doesn't change with changing. By changing without changing, I'm moved by the Great Oneness and carried in its unfolding order. And because of what doesn't change, I'm unaffected by everything that does change.

"So I drift and wander, and I follow the selfless urges that arise from deep within myself. And somehow — wherever I am — I find my proper place in the Great Oneness. When I'm moved and carried within an order that I recognize, I'm never lost. When all changing occurs within a wisdom that's not my own, then I'm satisfied with whatever happens."

Choosing

The Teaching:

The best choosing is selfless and thoughtless. Without the effort and struggle of decisions, choosing simply happens. Within everything's moving and shifting, circumstances change, timing finds its own time, and decisions make themselves. Trust wisdom's becoming. Follow its invisible unfolding. Without even choosing to choose, enter the grace of each moment's arriving.

The Commentary:

"When I'm walking along a street in Ch'ang-an or a path in the Wu Valley," said Old Shu, "I meet people. Sometimes they stop and ask, 'Hey, Old Shu, how are you? Where are you going?' I don't know what to say because I don't think about these things. So I just smile politely.

"How can I answer such questions when I don't know how I am or where I'm going? These are their questions, not mine. I am how I am. I go where I go. Who am I to decide such things? When I'm walking, I just walk. When I'm going, I just go. My body thoughtlessly breathes its breathing, my legs thoughtlessly move beneath me. With a lightness too light to measure and an easiness too easy to notice, I just thoughtlessly am. So how can I answer their questions?

"I go without knowing where I'm going, and I am without knowing who I am. I stay attentive, ever mindful and alert. But I don't interfere with the wisdom of the Great Oneness by trying to choose. Something that's not me chooses where I go and what I do. Something that's bigger than myself guides my wanderings. So I go without choosing. I move without moving. I travel a way that's not my own. I wander but I'm never lost.

"In the village market someone says, 'Ah, it's Old Shu. Here's some fruit. Would you like this bruised melon or this withered orange?' Or someone else asks, 'Would you like these wilted vegetables or a stale rice cake?' How am I to decide when I don't have preferences, when I eat everything with equal pleasure? How am I to choose with thoughts I don't have? So I just smile again, and they choose for me.

"When I'm at ease with the Great Oneness and contented with whatever it offers, how can I choose? I need air to breathe so the Great Oneness gives me the boundless sky. I need a place to stand so the Great Oneness gives me the solid land. I need water to drink so the Great Oneness gives me rain and cool mountain streams. What is the need for choosing?

"So I don't choose. When I'm looking, my eyes see what they see. When I'm hearing, my ears hear what they hear. I find food when I'm hungry and I find water when I'm thirsty. When I'm walking, my feet take me where they go and I just follow them. When I'm thinking, my thoughts think what they think so that's what I understand. Whatever happens to me is what happens. So from moment to peaceful moment I'm carried from wonder to boundless wonder. Why should I choose when I have what I need? And who am I to refuse what the Great Oneness offers?

"When I'm carried by the wisdom of becoming and I'm moved by the grace of each moment—when I want nothing but what I have—then what am I to choose? And when I accept whatever happens and I welcome whatever comes, then how am I to choose?"

Compassion

The Teaching:

Compassion does not question or doubt the unfolding order of wholeness. What happens has already happened. So be entirely present. Meet each moment with the clarity of calm attention. Stay balanced and quietly silent. Trust the wisdom of each unfolding moment. With acceptance as the only measure of judgment, let all the burdens of caring fall away. Then, from the distance of an immediate closeness, the fullness of the present is experienced as compassion. In the tranquility of an inner peace, compassion becomes timeless and boundless, moved yet unmoved in the stillness of both joy and sorrow.

The Commentary:

"To find compassion," said Old Shu, "I begin without compassion. I'm not overcome by the tragedy or suffering in the world. Life is dangerous and it always ends in death.

"So without a care about anyone or anything—without even a concern for myself—I summon my dragon strength. By breathing myself out, I breathe everything else in. And as I become smaller and smaller, everything else becomes larger and larger until the person I call Old Shu disappears into the Great Oneness. Then I see things exactly as they are, without the presence of myself to disturb the clarity.

"Without the shape of a self, I'm everywhere and nowhere. I'm the becoming and the passing of all things. I'm born and I'm old. I'm young and I'm dying. In my birth is the pain of joy and laughter. In my death is the comfort of grief and sorrow.

"I look beyond bliss and suffering. I see beyond delight and death. I behold order arising from chaos and chaos returning to order. I'm empty and I'm full. I'm silent and I speak. I'm someone and I'm no one. I'm man and I'm woman. I'm full and yet I'm empty, serenely alive in the wonder of all that happens.

"Below my feet is the tumult of a living Earth. Above my neckbone is the calm of an endless Heaven. And I'm in the full middle, fully aware yet untouched, undisturbed and unmoved by wisdom's compassion.

"And then, as if I were nothing, all the tears of weeping and all the laughters of joy pass through the belly and the bones of my body, rise into the gentle circle of an enclosing sky, and are received into the grace of boundless silence."

Conjoining

The Teaching:

The urge that brings man and woman together overcomes their separateness. In the boundless moment of their meeting, they become a moving oneness, living and dying in the fullness of each other. Where is man and where is woman when the two are one? Where are differences when togetherness is dancing its timeless promise of fulfilment? Where is self and other when both have become a single, urgent need rushing toward release? This is the thoughtless place where laughter and tears meet, the first and the last of all understanding. This is togetherness completing togetherness. It is body's release from body, the insistent moment that defies both birth and death.

The Commentary:

"I have a story to tell," said Old Shu, "but I'm not going to tell it. The story has a beginning but I don't know what it is. Maybe the young women of the brothel made a playful bet with each other, or maybe they intended their meeting with me to be a joke. It isn't important. But what began in silly giggles ended in tears of deep joy. And Old Shu became the lover of one of these lovers.

"How is this possible? Men and women are different yet the same. When a man finds his own wholeness, he can speak to a woman with the part of himself that they share. Then he can tell her of the magic of their differences and the promise that is greater than their separateness.

"How is this done? First I become one with her so she can become one with me. This is the beginning of our understanding. When I can see myself in her, she can see herself in me. So, we find something more than each other. Besides, she's a woman and I'm a man so we fit together. I teach her my skills and she teaches me hers. Then, by following the wisdom of nature, we fulfil each other.

"Sometimes I mount her or sometimes she mounts me—it doesn't matter. Sometimes we're together as lovers, sometimes as animals—this doesn't matter, either.

"When we're together as lovers, I'm only aware of her body so I become selfless, satisfying only her. She, too, is selfless, satisfying only me. Because each of us is only aware of the other's body, we overcome our separateness and thereby reach togetherness. Then we move as one body. And when we've finished, we're both at peace with our bodies, with each other and with the Great Oneness.

"When we're together as animals, we trust each other so we can both release to primal desire. Then I disappear as myself, she disappears as herself, and we both become the same thoughtless urgency rushing toward release. Because we're the same and we're no longer different, we move together as one body. And when we've finished and we return to our separate selves, we're both at peace with our bodies, with each other and with the Great Oneness.

"As lovers, she finds more than her womanhood by losing it to me, and I find more than my manhood by losing it to her. As animals, she finds more than herself by losing herself, and I find more than myself by losing myself.

"At first, a man and a woman are like guests in each other's houses—the duty of the man is to bring the woman's body to satisfaction, and the duty of the woman is to bring the man's body to satisfaction. When they finally dwell in the same house, they can forget that they're a separate man and woman. The attraction of body for body is just the urge that brings them to each other, to be together what they cannot be alone. Then, with a gentle discipline, they'll find what's greater than themselves."

Crisis

The Teaching:

Crisis is the meeting of danger and opportunity. Disorder threatens but new order arises. When the breaking of the old becomes the beginning of the new, balance is tested. The prospects smile with risk and uncertainty. Crisis is not the time for preparation or desperate searching. Circumstances change quickly so existing resources are summoned and inner balance is maintained. Bend and yield in the face of adversity but remain inwardly strong and peaceful. Respect the insights that are honed from seasoned experience, the clarity that comes spontaneously from the quiet centre within. Trust the unfolding wisdom that guides all change. Attention that is calm and unwavering will find a way through the urgency of crisis.

The Commentary:

"Even though a stream begins in the mountains," said Old Shu, "it ends in the sea. Sometimes it flows quickly and sometimes it flows slowly. But it's always itself. And it always takes a downward course to fulfil its destiny.

"Birth has brought me to a life where death is inevitable, so why should I be concerned about dangers and disasters. The worst they can do is complete what life has promised.

"The Great Oneness turns and churns within itself, changing everything but changing nothing. So why should I get excited about matters of life or death, about a wholeness that's always whole?

"When danger looms or disaster strikes, I remember the strength within myself, the quickness and the slowness of my downward journey to the sea. In different circumstances I move in different ways. But, no matter how I move, I'm always true to my inner nature.

"And what's my inner nature? It's the silent weight that holds me to the rocks of the mountain and the soil of the valley, the downward pull that calls me to the sea. Because my life is unfolding within the wisdom of the Great Oneness, I'm carried where and how I ought to go. Sometimes I'm swift as rapids and sometimes I'm calm as pools. But I'm always myself—always moving as easily as a stream moves, always right with wherever I am.

"How do I know when to move quickly or slowly? The same way I know whether my life will be long or short. Since these things are beyond my knowing, I don't ask questions or search for answers. I just release to whatever happens and enter the circumstances that arise. When I stay true to my inner nature—when I'm calm and unafraid—then the circumstances tell me what to do.

"Like water moving to destiny's urge, I meet whatever comes. Danger, disaster, hunger, cold—all these things arise and pass away. I just follow my downward course amid the hard stones and soft mosses, amid the bending grasses and searching roots. A way opens and I'm drawn into it. I sigh and whisper, I bubble and chuckle. I even laugh and cry. But moment by magic moment, I'm always where I belong. So crisis has nothing to do with me."

Death

The Teaching:

From nowhere and everywhere, something familiar yet unknown calls to the living body. With unfailing reply, the body weakens and wearies, withers and falters. Then its still centre goes out of balance and death takes back what life has given. For those who are seekers of answers, life and death are the same question. Since such questions arise from mystery and return to mystery, the last answer is always silence. So words sound hollow in the shadowed company of death. And they are spoken, not to inform, but to comfort. The thin echo of their solace searches through the sorry veil of grief to say what is beyond saying. Therefore, the distant words that are offered to the bereaved can only affirm that the living are still alive, still breathing the delicate wonder that is more than silence can speak.

The Commentary:

"Life is for the living," said Old Shu, "and death is for the dead. Since the living are not dead and the dead are not living, let those who are alive be concerned with the things of life and let those who are dead be concerned with the things of death. When I'm living, I'll attend to the things of life. When I'm dead, the things of death will attend to themselves.

"When the living can't even understand life, how are they supposed to understand death? Death is a changing that's more than thoughts can think so I don't worry about it. Still, death affects life. And old age is not the same as youth. How can it be otherwise when the seed of death enters the body at birth?

"Even though I'm undisturbed by the promise of death—even though I look inward and find my selfless centre unchanged—I'm not the same as when I was young. Once I saw the world as a clever opponent to be challenged. Now I see it as a faithful friend to be honoured. So I pay more attention to the wisdom of its changing. And I listen more carefully as the music

72

of each season fills open valleys and covers high mountains. I'm still peacefully quiet, still serenely full of the wonders of life, but I experience them differently — more slowly and appreciatively, holding them longer and more tenderly in each passing moment.

"So here I stand in the lateness of this day, my bent body warmed by the soft blessing of an afternoon sun and my aging hair tussled by a cool breeze. My weathered skin, as parched as dried river mud, welcomes the touch of the world. And I smile as my body grows more upside-down every day, taking me headfirst into the ground.

"And what's the blessing of this? Hah! When everyone else stands straight and tall, they look up to Heaven. When I stand straight and tall, I look down to Earth. The older I get, the closer my nose gets to the bottom of my feet. Other people can forget about death. For me, it looms closer every day. Now, wherever I walk, I can smell the fallen pine needles and the scattered rice straw, the moist humus and the waiting clay. When death comes, I'll be ready.

"Someday this form that's called Old Shu will go out of balance. His body will return to the ground and join the living soil; his breath will be taken by the wind and enter the invisible air; his thoughts will pass into the unknown and become one with the Great Oneness. So he'll find in his death what he's been seeking in his life.

"Search for Old Shu — you won't find him in his present form. But he won't disappear. Where can he go? When he was alive, he was somewhere. When he's dead, he'll be everywhere. So he'll be easy to find. Look, and you'll see him in the bending curve of a river, in the crooked branch of a pine, in the twisted stem of a mulberry. Listen, and you'll hear him in the splashing of a mountain stream, in the dripping of dew-drenched mosses, in the whispering fall of snowflakes. Become quiet enough and maybe you'll hear his thoughts filling the empty silence of a dark night, or his dreams singing to the cool stillness of a white moon.

"In death, I'll go where I have to go. What else can I do? What else can happen? My bones grew from the waiting stones and my flesh arose from the living soil. My blood is the flowing water of streams and rivers, my thoughts are the wind and air of a great breathing. So in death I'll return to my source, and I'll

73

become what I always was. That's where I began, so that's where I'll end. What could be a better ending? And as for me, I won't mind being nowhere and everywhere, at one with the Great Oneness."

Doing

The Teaching:

When thoughts stop interfering with doing, doing does itself. Without the confusion of thoughts, all the clutter of consideration and judgment no longer disturbs the ease of each moment's unfolding. Body is free to respond with its wisdom. The senses return to their nameless clarity. Seeing simply sees. Hearing simply hears. Then thoughtless doing moves in accord with the wholeness of things. When doing no longer pauses for questions or doubts, each moment overflows with the fullness of itself, too complete to allow for hesitation.

The Commentary:

"Whatever I do," said Old Shu, "I do without doing. How do I do without doing? In the morning I sleep until I awake. The rest of the day is the same. I just do what I do until I do something else. Is this too difficult to understand?

"Since no one can do nothing, I'm always doing something. So even when I seem to be doing nothing, I'm open and alert, clear and attentive, peacefully waiting until I move. Then when I move, I move until I stop. When I'm going, I just go — but I don't know where I'm going. And when I stop, I just stop — but I don't know when I'll start again. Maybe this is too simple to understand. When I'm tired, I rest. When I'm hungry, I eat. When I'm thirsty, I drink. By following the directions of each moment, I just do what I do.

"How do I know what to do? I wait for what's inside to respond to what's outside. I attend to the impulses that arise from the quietness within myself, from the thoughtless place that's not the thinking me. Somewhere, deep inside, there's a silent centre, a stillness where the outside world seems to gather itself. So I listen to this silent stillness. But I don't hear words or even thoughts. Instead, I follow the gentle urges that arise within me. Guided by each moment's impulse, I move in harmony with everything that's not me.

"I don't know how this happens. I don't try to understand. I don't even think about it. But I feel a wholeness and a balance in myself. And I feel a wholeness and a balance in the world. I sense the way I'm moving in this wholeness and I sense the way this wholeness is moving in me. Then I keep them both together — the inside and the outside — balanced with each other in the stillness of each moment.

"This requires a disciplined presence. One missed moment and I lose the direction that guides me. So I pay careful attention to exactly where I am, accepting every new moment exactly as it is. Then I just do what I do, without any thought of what I'm doing.

"People see me and think I'm lost and confused, that I'm just wandering aimlessly. It's true that I don't know where I'm going. And I may be confused. But I'm never lost."

Earth

The Teaching:

Once the obvious is lost, the search to find it is long and arduous. Even with nothing else to know and nowhere else to belong, the one easy answer is elusive. The obvious and the profound are difficult to find because they are each other. The simple and the ordinary are the last to be recognized because they are the beginning and the ending of all journeys. But travel far enough and the roundness of searching will return every question to the same answer. Everything worth knowing is in the living wisdom of a fragile beauty that will always have its way.

The Commentary:

"I want to say something," said Old Shu, "but I don't know how to say it. So I'll just begin and maybe I'll say what I want to say.

"Wherever I go, I've never been able to escape mountains and valleys, hills and rivers, fields and forests. I look and I see stones and trees. I listen and I hear wind and rain. When I breathe, I smell grasses and flowers. The living air touches my skin with the comfort of warmth and the sting of cold. Cool streams sing me water-songs. A thousand shades of green enliven each budding spring. And winter crows shine absurdly black on frozen ponds.

"All this is more amazing than amazing. It floods my senses to overflowing and I nearly burst with the wonder of it. So I'm always filled with endless awe, overcome by more blessings than counting can count. The land is firm and honest beneath my feet. The sky wraps me in its soft embrace. The days enrich me and the nights rest me. So, wherever I am, I'm always where I belong, always at home.

"And everything I know, I've learned from being where I am. I know what's great because of Mount Shan towering into clouds. I know what's delicate because of beaded dew on morning cobwebs. I know what's wet when sudden cloudbursts drench rice paddies, and what's dry when hot rocks muffle cricket-calls. Dancing butterflies teach me freedom. Winter storms show me power. Falling petals instruct me on loss and acceptance. So I listen while rustling leaves and silent fog tell me their secrets. And after the chill of winter has strengthened me with its discipline, the cheer of summer consoles me with its kindness. This is why I am who I am, how I know what I know.

"But whatever I am and for all I know, I can't explain all these things that shape me and teach me and fill my senses. They just are—as close and mysterious as my own breathing.

"Am I the only one who sees that the ordinary is extraordinary? Isn't anyone else overcome by the wonder of it? Is everyone else too busy and distracted to be amazed, to feel what I feel?

"I can't imagine being anywhere else but here, alive and aware in the richness of this place. This is what is. This is all I know. This is where I belong. This is who I am.

"The rain and trees, the grass and clouds—all these ordinary things that are everywhere—they're me. And I'm all these things. We're each other. How can it be otherwise? My bones are the dust of stones and my flesh is the soil of fields. My blood is the water of rivers and my breath is the wind of sky blowing gently within me. Even my waking and sleeping is the rhythm of days and nights. And all these separate parts belong to one wholeness, one living body divided only by forgetting.

"So I remember. This is why I have to say what I say. I can't shout like cracking thunder or whisper like falling snow, so I have to speak with the words that I can speak."

Easiness

The Teaching:

Easiness arises from the strength of inner discipline and the resilience of inner strength. When discipline and strength have replaced stubborn willfulness, then resilience will find openings in each moment's unfolding and an easy becoming will replace obstacles and struggle. When waiting, just wait. Be relaxed and ready. Without wishing or wanting, without dreaming or desiring, without even hoping or expecting, accept each unfolding moment as itself. Be at peace with whatever happens. Do not be afraid. Trust the nameless place where the inner and the outer are each other. When a stillness pervades all changing, even the difficult becomes easy. Because easiness arises from inner discipline and inner strength, it must first pass through the challenge of difficulty.

The Commentary:

"Rivers flow between mountains and through valleys," said Old Shu, " always moving into the lowest place. Water knows about openings so it always follows the easiest course.

"When I move, I move between obstacles and I follow the downward course of things. When I'm not moving, I wait patiently, always ready for the opening that invites me into itself. Then, when this opening calls, I move without hesitation. But I never know what I'll do or where I'll go until each opening presents itself.

"Because the Great Oneness unfolds as it will, who am I to know what will happen or what to do? There's a time to do each thing but, until it comes, who knows when it will be? And there's a way to do each thing but, until it reveals itself, who knows what it is?

"Because each situation is itself, I begin as if it has nothing to do with me. If I think I know what it will be, or when it will be or what I'll do, my expectation interferes with my action and my timing. If I were foolish enough to be guided by my expectations, I'd be out of harmony with every situation that arises.

"When I'm wholly attentive and without expectations—when I've found a quiet readiness within myself—I'm at one with each unfolding moment and in balance with the circumstances that arrive. Then I can feel the openings that invite me to enter, I can follow the yielding that allows me to move, and I can sense the wisdom that keeps me in harmony with the Great Oneness.

"Obstacles disappear while opportunities arise and present themselves. A way opens before me and I'm welcomed into each new moment. Wherever I am, I belong. And like the flowing of water, I'm drawn forever downward along an effortless course."

Emptiness

The Teaching:

All the imagined parts of wholeness appear and disappear in the fullness of becoming and passing away. Everything changes but the emptiness at the deepest centre is undisturbed by all that happens. Since each thing arises from emptiness and returns to emptiness, become the beginning and the ending of all that is, the first and the last of all that will be. Empty until silence finds its place in stillness. Without names or differences, without questions or answers, without certainty or self, become lost in the formless and the timeless. When silence resides peacefully in stillness, hearing will hear itself and seeing will see itself, feeling will feel itself and thinking will think itself. Then emptiness will be full, and everything will be the same as before—yet different.

The Commentary:

"I want to say something about nothing," said Old Shu. "This nothing isn't exactly nothing. But it isn't something, either. I know I can't say what it is and I know I can't think what it is because it's between all words and thoughts, between all the separate parts of things that words and thoughts invent. But I can feel it between my words and my thoughts so I have to say something about it.

"Between all the separate parts of things, there's an emptiness that separates one thing from another and holds the fullness of everything that is. And this emptiness is a special nothing.

"Because this nothing contains everything, it must be boundless and shapeless, timeless and formless. It allows changing to change and lets becoming become itself. It holds mountains and valleys, rivers and seas. It holds the sky and moon, the sun and stars. And it also holds me and all the things I think and feel.

"I can't understand this emptiness but I can feel it as a place that holds me. I can feel my body moving in it, my eyes seeing in it, my thoughts thinking in it.

"Beyond everything I am, there's a place where I'm not. Beyond the reach of my biggest thoughts, there's an empty place where I can no longer think. When I'm beyond the reach of myself and my biggest thoughts, then I come to the edge of this emptiness and I fall into the vastness of a special becoming that's more than anything I can think or feel.

"Emptiness is always inviting me to become more than I am. So whenever I lose this special sense of becoming — whenever I fill with certainties that close my inner openness — I empty so I can receive what's more than myself. Although I'm filled with the fullness of each moment, I stay balanced and aware, alert and ready, forever entering the welcome unfolding of this emptiness. That's how I meet everything that happens. That's how I know more than I can understand, and how I become more than I am."

Endings

The Teaching:

The past fulfils itself in the present, beginnings fulfil themselves in endings, and endings fulfil themselves in new beginnings. Although endings and beginnings are called by different names, they arise from each other and are the same. Those who need differences and the burden of effort will always invent endings and beginnings. But those who do not need differences can surrender them and enter the easiness of an endless becoming. Then they will find an undivided fullness without the distinctions that disturb the arrival of a timeless now.

The Commentary:

"If every moment is an ending," said Old Shu, "then I know when beginnings begin. And I know when the old completes itself and when the new starts. If every moment is a beginning, then I know when endings arrive, when the new becomes old and when things complete themselves.

"But if every moment is both an ending and a beginning, why should I pay attention to either? Aren't the mountain streams of summer the melting snows of winter? And aren't the blowing seeds of autumn the sprouting greens of spring? If endings and beginnings are the same — just different parts of one wholeness — then what's the need for distinctions? So I forget about them and I pay attention to exactly where I am.

"By staying where I am, I move with everything that moves and I change with everything that changes. I cultivate my inner stillness and I keep my balance. When I'm still and balanced, I'm peaceful. When I'm peaceful, I'm timeless. When I'm timeless, I'm patient. And when I'm patient, I'm unhurried and calm. Then I'm always attentive and ready. Regardless of what happens, I just stay where I am — alert and present, poised on the edge of each moment's becoming, following the course of an unfolding grace.

"In this unfolding grace, endings and beginnings flow into each other, moving effortlessly together with an unbroken ease.

"Most people like to separate endings from beginnings and struggle with differences. But I don't. So I just smile, think my own thoughts and follow the endless way that opens before me. These are my endings. And these are my beginnings, too."

Following

The Teaching:

Enter the unfolding order of wholeness by following its downward course. Meet each moment with inner balance. Cultivate discipline until discipline's strength learns how to yield. Trust until all struggle disappears and yielding's acceptance becomes a stillness. Enter this stillness and move with its moving. Discover the grace of its becoming. Without the burdens of intention or self, find the way that finds itself. With attention fully present and with trust undisturbed, follow the unfolding order into the wisdom of each moment.

The Commentary:

"A mountain stream," said Old Shu, "splashes over rock and swirls between stones. Sometimes it flows quickly and sometimes it flows slowly, tumbling and winding its downward course to the valley below. Even though it doesn't know where it's going, it always goes where it's supposed to go.

"It's the same with me. There's something that pulls me where I'm supposed to go, that takes me along a course I have to travel. I don't know where I'm going and I don't know why. So I just go where I go, drawn by the urge that invites me downward.

"At first, when I was a child, I was too young to remember that I was at one with the Great Oneness. And when I became a young man, I was too willful to know I was still at one with the Great Oneness. Because I was youthful and stubborn, I had to work and struggle, to use my strength and discipline to get what I wanted. Why? Because I was trying to become myself, to reach my belonging in the vast mystery that held me in its care. I couldn't trust so I couldn't see what was opening before me. I couldn't let go so I couldn't release to the Great Oneness and follow the downward course of its wisdom.

"Now, by accepting rather than struggling, I use a

different kind of strength and discipline. The strength is soft and the discipline is yielding. By connecting whatever's inside me to whatever's outside me, I'm no longer just myself. So I follow what I don't understand and I move without purpose. I no longer have a beginning or an ending so I'm ancient and timeless. Everything that happens to me is both old and new, both remembered and unfamiliar. And by some strange magic of the mountain, the someone who's called Old Shu always arrives where he belongs."

Forgetting

The Teaching:

Forgetting is the cleansing that allows the freshness of each new moment to be received in the fullness of itself. Without the burden of the past, the present can be met exactly as it is. To meet each new moment, trust the remembering that dwells deeper than memory, the wisdom that began before learning was born. It recalls what needs to be recalled and it remembers what cannot be forgotten. And do not forget that forgetting is a special way of forgiving.

The Commentary:

"The more I forget the past," said Old Shu, "the more clearly I enter the present. How can I travel lightly today when I'm packing the baggage of yesterday? Forgetting frees me to be where I am, to meet the simple clarity of each new moment.

"So I forget and I empty. I open and I receive. I wander aimlessly and the grace of the Great Oneness carries me from moment to passing moment, from place to peaceful place. The sun shines and the rain falls. The seasons follow upon seasons. But I'm just where I am, moving in a welcoming stillness, lost in the wonder of whatever happens.

"Because I don't understand and I don't remember, my centre is undisturbed and I'm inwardly quiet. So I meet and I accept whatever comes, and then I let go and I forget whatever passes.

"By forgetting, I become no one and everyone. I'm everywhere and I'm nowhere — suspended between changing and unchanging, balanced on the edge of a vast unfolding that moves but is always still. I'm captive but I'm also free. I'm ancient but I'm also young, forever fresh and alive in the wonder of a timeless mystery.

"Because I don't remember where I've been and I don't know where I'm going, I follow each moment's urge. And as I'm lifted and carried by the grace of the Great Oneness, the fullness of each moment overcomes me. And so I receive the delight of new joys and the weight of new sorrows — all of them ready to be forgotten."

Giving

The Teaching:

Giving that arises from itself asks for nothing, takes nothing and then returns to nothing. When it comes spontaneously from the wholeness of each moment's need, those who give and those who receive are both honoured. Giving becomes a selfless receiving and receiving becomes a selfless giving. Then givers are not burdened with the weight of their generosity and receivers are not burdened with the weight of their gratitude. So a freedom releases both givers and receivers into the fullness of each moment's unfolding.

The Commentary:

"When I give," said Old Shu, "I don't give things—I don't even give myself. As each situation arises, I feel my place in the wholeness of the moment and I move with its unfolding. Then I forget who I am and something that's not me responds to whatever's happening. Each situation asks me to do what I don't expect. And then a giving—a giving that has nothing to do with me—just offers itself.

"Sometimes I meet people walking alone on a path or in a quiet place in the village. If the feelings inside them are too big to contain, they stop to talk. 'Old Shu,' they ask, 'How are you?' And then they tell me about themselves.

"Maybe they talk to me because they think I'm strange and I'll understand the strangeness that's in them. Maybe they talk to me because I look different and they think I don't belong in their world. Then they say what they need to say without fear that I'll tell anyone. Maybe they tell me of their inner pain because my body is misshapen and they think I'm their companion in suffering. Maybe they tell me of their inner happiness because my eyes are smiling and they think I'm their companion in joy. People see what they see, find what they find and do what they do.

"So they tell me about their hopes and fears, about their victories and sorrows. Sometimes they lay the weight of their secrets upon my neckbone and laugh or cry as if they're laughing or crying to themselves. I just listen quietly and patiently.

"The best thing to give to people is themselves. So I cultivate my silence so they can hear what they're saying, my emptiness so they can receive what they're feeling, my stillness so they can find what they're seeking. Then they each can be comfortable, accepting and honest with who they are.

"Because of my silence and emptiness and stillness, the weight of their burdens and secrets upon me are as light as passing breezes. Although I'm moved by their feelings, I'm unaffected. Although I'm filled by their thoughts, I'm alone. Because of my separateness, I can be truly close. Because of my indifference, I can be truly caring.

"When I'm still and silent, people use me like a tree to regain their balance. When I'm still and undisturbed, they use me like a mirror to see themselves. When I'm still and empty, they use me like the sky to find the beginning of their own peace.

"Maybe people come to me because of what I'm not—and when they're ready to talk to themselves, they talk to me instead. Because I never judge, they think I understand. Because I just listen and ask questions, they find the answers they already know. Maybe that's how they find their own wholeness. And when they feel better, they go on their way.

"So I give by receiving. By accepting what happens and by moving with the natural order, I don't disturb the Great Oneness. And because my emptiness is always empty and my fullness is always full, I'm free to go my own way, unburdened by the weight of either giving or receiving."

Grace

The Teaching:

Grace is wholeness moving within the stillness of itself. Without separateness to disturb the unfolding order, without effort or struggle—without even purpose—the generosity of each moment becomes the fullness of the next. Once acceptance has calmed desire and trust has quieted doubt, then purpose finds its own way as grace. Therefore, become the undivided wholeness that is the grace of wisdom's unfolding. Forget yesterday. Do not consider tomorrow. Meet each moment as it arises. Do not hurry. Because grace moves with its own ease, let quickness and slowness find themselves. Do not use force. Wait patiently when resistance is encountered. Move gently within everything's moving. Cultivate softness, simplicity and a gentle strength. Always be mindful of each situation's wholeness. Since grace is each moment moving in balance with wholeness, do not stop to examine it and do not try to explain it.

The Commentary:

"I've found something that isn't mine," said Old Shu. "Maybe it doesn't belong to anyone. Maybe no one lost it. I don't know what it is and I don't know what to call it. Maybe it's something or maybe it's nothing at all.

"Whatever it is, it seems to be a way of moving with the order of things so that inside and outside are each other, so that separateness and togetherness are the same.

"If I were to give it a name, I'd call it grace. But this is just a word. I could call it another name but no word will say what it is. Therefore, I forget distinctions so I don't invite difficulties. And I forget myself so I don't create resistance. And then I let the secret wisdom of the Great Oneness happen of itself.

"How can I explain how this happens when it has nothing to do with me? The wisdom just finds its own wisdom—not because of what I do but because of what I don't do. So I just let go and I yield to the wholeness that's greater than myself. When I don't interfere, the way finds itself. And I just follow the path that opens before me.

"Now I've started to say something that may not be sayable, and I've started to explain something that may not be explainable. Maybe I should stop right here before I cause any more confusion. But I've got something else to say so I might as well try to say it.

"A grain of sand is as heavy as the towering weight of Mount Shan and a drop of rain is as vast as the empty sky above Emperor Yao's kingdom. Anyone who understands this will know that simplicity must pass through complexity to become truly simple, that easiness must pass through difficulty to become truly easy. Even greatness is not truly great until it becomes humble and ordinary.

"What do I mean? I mean that I can't let go of the world until I take hold of it, that I can't lose myself until I find myself. If I want the certainty of knowing, I have to be overcome by the uncertainty of confusion. If I want the easiness of grace, I have to master the strictness of discipline.

"And I have this to say, too. Just as there's inside and outside, there's up and down. Just as there's light and dark, there's fullness and emptiness. Just as there's everything and nothing, there's Old Shu and there's no Old Shu. And when all these differences become each other, this someone called Old Shu enters the stillness at the very centre of wholeness. And that's when grace finds him."

Grief

The Teaching:

The grace of birth burdens each life with the weight of death. For those still living, the trusting heart that once welcomed the offered sweets of wanted joy must now receive the ashen bitters of imposed sorrow. Grief is laughter's other voice. Using the same tears for a different purpose, grief takes away what laughter gives. So cry the silent flood of sorrow that speaks what words cannot say. Allow the heavy ache in bones to suffer their own slow grief. Accept the bewildered thoughts that are unable to see beyond the end of loss. And while the saddened heart beats its long way back to broken peace, remember the nameless and unmoving centre that watches the distant pain of mourning. Amid the becoming and passing of all things, this quiet stillness keeps the constant balance that endures from birth to death. Lighter than breath and stronger than bone, it endures beyond grief.

The Commentary:

"Once I had a wife," said Old Shu. "And when she died, my body felt like I would die, too. My mind understood that everything living must die so it accepted her death. From a place of quiet calm, it could see the rising and falling of all things — the vast order of coming and going that changes but does not change. My mind found solace in what it knew but could not understand.

"But my body knew her differently so it had its own kind of grief. It cried because its eyes had become a well of tears and its flesh a place of sorrow. Since my body also loved my wife, it too had its say.

"Because my body and my mind received her death differently, they became divided from each other. So, for a while, I lost my wholeness.

I clearly remember everything that happened but my grief

made each moment seem far away, as if it were happening to someone else. And all the sharpness of my seeing seemed dull and slow, stiff and heavy, as if my awareness had separated from itself. My mind watched from a distance while my poor body ached and my sad heart drummed its throbbing sorrow. Then the tears finally washed away the grief and I was whole again.

"But that was many years ago. And I was changed by what happened. Grief taught me that something beyond value had been lost. Then it taught me that something beyond understanding had been found. So the old emptiness left by death was filled with a new wisdom learned from life.

"Breath comes from wind and flesh from soil. Bones arise from stone and return to dust. In the long grace of slow time, lives come and then they go. Since this is what is and what must be, I'll be contented."

Heaven

The Teaching:

The present falls away in each moment's passing and an opening appears at the very edge of becoming. Between what is and what will be lies the fullness of Heaven. So do not search far away for what is closer than near. Do not waste hopes on hoping or wishes on wishing. Dreams are only the substance of dreaming. With the peaceful discipline of inner strength and the empty readiness of silent balance, enter the unfolding wisdom of each moment's arriving. Heaven's grace is so close it almost eludes finding.

The Commentary:

"People tell me," said Old Shu, "that the priests of the Tien-po Temple talk about the realms of Heaven and Earth. But I don't know about such things. How would I know which is Heaven and which is Earth when I'm just where I am?

"But I remember that I used to wish and dream. I used to believe in fancy ideas and big thoughts. I used to think that if I thought hard enough I could understand important things. So I asked endless questions and I searched wherever my asking took me. But I couldn't find anywhere else but where I was.

"At first, when I was being defeated by fancy ideas and big thoughts, I felt puzzled and lost. Everything I knew seemed silly and meaningless, as if the hope inside myself were falling away and all the comfort of my wishes and dreams were emptying into an abyss of confusion. How was I to understand important things if I couldn't think the right thoughts?

"Then a strange thing began to happen. Without wishing or wanting, without dreaming or thinking—without even the effort of trying—I began to fill with a carefree lightness, a thoughtless clarity and a comfortable simplicity. So I stopped searching. And I became peacefully fulfilled, like I'd arrived at the end of a long journey.

"Maybe this is what the priests mean when they talk about Heaven. I don't know. I'm still here, the same as before—but now I'm different. I've become contented and easy with everything that happens, as if I'm held in the careful embrace of a deep and inner stillness. And from this stillness I see who I am. I see my thoughts thinking themselves. And I see the completeness of things moving but not moving, changing but not changing.

"Now I don't wish or dream. I don't try to think like the priests of the temple or the scholars of Emperor Yao's court. Complex things have become simple again. Questions have disappeared. I don't search for answers. I don't struggle. What I think and what I do just happens to me. So I move but I don't move, I change but I don't change.

"And I have something else to say that might have something to do with Heaven.

"Now, wherever I move, there's an opening in front of me. And whenever I change, there's a spaciousness that invites me into whatever's next. I'm aware but I don't think. I'm lost in a vast mystery yet I'm found in a great wonder. Because I'm just wherever I am, I'm unhurried and timeless. Behind me is the disappearing moment of what's happened. Ahead of me is the unfolding promise of what's to come. Between what was and what will be is the fullness of a living present. And that's Heaven enough for me."

Humility

The Teaching:

Wealth cannot buy contentment and force cannot win affection. Greed cannot hoard serenity and ambition cannot escape death. Because death will always have its way, even the richest and the most powerful must return to the wisdom of dust. So what is pride in the company of death? And what are the shining adornments of vanity, pretension, vengeance and honour? Those who know the limits of mortality have found the secret of humility. Those who discover riches in the ordinary have earned the greatest wealth. And those who dwell peacefully with the commonplace have attained the highest dignity and claimed a timeless treasure.

The Commentary:

"From my poor hut," said Old Shu, "I see the same magic moon as Emperor Yao. The plain water I drink would quench his thirst. On my wrinkled face, I feel the same warming sun as his handsome courtiers. And my little accomplishments bring as much satisfaction to me as the victories of his conquering generals.

"I have no strong bearers to carry me in a golden chair, no noble horses to pull me in a gilded carriage, no dutiful soldiers to clear my way on crowded streets. But the welcoming world opens and receives me like an honoured guest as I freely walk the valley paths and mountain slopes.

"My contentment is as deep as those who are rich, as satisfying as those who are accomplished, as valuable as those who are acclaimed. And what would I do with fame when my laughter and joy already fill me to overflowing?

"For people as poor as Old Shu, the rush of a spring wind is still fresh, the ringing of a birdsong still tingles the air, the unclouded sight of a starry sky is still mysteriously huge. When my simple senses bring me boundless delight, what more could I want than the few treasures I have?

"Because I'm unimportant, I'm not noticed by those of importance. Because I have no wealth to guard, no pride to protect, no honour to defend, I go freely on my way, unburdened by the weight of my person. The powerful don't challenge me to prove their might. The vain don't envy me to feed their jealousy. The scheming don't pester me to win my influence.

"Because of what I'm not, the world is at ease with me and I'm at ease with the world. So we're at peace with each other."

Impeccability

The Teaching:

Grace does not begin as grace and easiness does not begin as easiness. In the beginning, simplicity is lost in complexity and clarity is hidden in confusion. Accomplishments are first attained with effort and success is earned with struggle that threatens balance. After skills have been studied, practiced and mastered, they can be forgotten. Then their outer form falls away and their inner power is manifest. When a quiet readiness waits patiently at the edge of each moment's becoming, all doing is guided by a thoughtless discipline. Then the difficult finally becomes easy and impeccability is attained.

The Commentary:

"I have a way of moving with the world so its harmony is not disturbed," said Old Shu. "Therefore, everything I do is disciplined. That's how I make the difficult easy, how I free myself from differences, and how I enter the harmony of the Great Oneness.

"People want the luck and the blessings of Heaven but they don't want the trouble of earning it. So they go to temples with offerings, burn joss sticks and pray on all the favourable days. They think there's a here and a there, an inside and an outside. They want good fortune but they want it bestowed upon them like a gift from Heaven.

"But the world is its own place and it works in its own way. If I follow its way, then it blesses me with grace. If I oppose its way, then it burdens me with trouble. So the art of my discipline teaches me how to move with the world—how to change with its changing and how to earn its generosity. Without asking, I receive what I need. Without desire, I get what I want. Without a self, I find my very own belonging.

"This is difficult to do because the Great Oneness is a

stern teacher. So, at first, I learn by being attentive and by making mistakes. Slowly, I hone the clarity of my thinking and the sharpness of my actions until they're too keen to find. When my discipline becomes easy and spontaneous, I'm like a sword that moves without being seen, like an arrow that releases without being shot, like a bowl that forms itself on the potter's wheel.

"Without attention or deliberate effort, my actions become one with the wholeness of each moment. Because I've entered the unfolding of the Great Oneness, I move in harmony with a wisdom that's not my own. Then, whatever I do, whatever I receive or whatever I accomplish, is not my own. And my impeccability doesn't belong to me."

Knowing

The Teaching:

The shape of answers cannot contain the greatness of questions. The smallness of self cannot hold the vastness of knowing. Since the formless overcomes form and the mysterious encloses the known, those with only questions and confusion are prepared and ready. When questions are deep enough to overcome asking and searching is earnest enough to confound thinking, uncertainty disappears into itself and the peace of a nameless knowing suddenly arises from the stillness of inward listening. Then something wordless and thoughtless speaks in the silence. A timeless clarity replaces questions and confusion. Although nothing changes, nothing is the same. Answers are no longer answers and questions are no longer questions. Everything's moving continues to move but the moving itself does not move. And all turmoil rises and falls within an empty stillness, within a wonder that is full beyond full.

The Commentary:

"If I know that I don't know," said Old Shu, "then I must know something that I don't know. And knowing something that I don't know is very important to know.

"Now, maybe I've said something or maybe I've said nothing. I don't know. But I know that I don't understand what I know. And I don't understand how I know what I don't understand. But something overcomes me — something that's more than thoughts can think — and this something fills me with a special kind of wordless knowing.

"This happen when I soften and I open. Then I begin to fill with the wonder of things. To make room for all this wonder, I empty of everything I am. And without an Old Shu, the world floods me with itself.

"Without an Old Shu, trees are still trees but they're no

longer shaped by the words that call them trees. Rivers and mountains and clouds are just what they are but they're no longer formed by the thoughts that make them something else. Everything is amazing and profound, brilliant and clear, simple and ordinary. And then what I know is so obvious that I'm surprised that I should even be surprised.

"But if I interfere with this knowing by offering anything of myself—my own ideas, my own thoughts, even my own feelings—I lose the emptiness that receives it. Then my thoughts become thick and heavy, and my body becomes large and awkward. I stumble instead of walking gracefully. I no longer have the balance and the timing that keeps me in harmony with the world around me.

"To find this knowing again, I mindlessly open and receive everything that enters me. I don't judge. I don't understand. I don't try to know. I just lose myself in the immensity of things. I become quiet and lost, insignificant and confused, overcome by the vastness of everything that is. Then something that's like nothing moves in me, rises through the confusion in me, and fills me with a thoughtless clarity— with a knowing that's not mine, with a fullness that's serenely and wonderfully still.

"I know but I forget that I know, so I never know what to say or do. But at the proper times, something finds me and guides me. Then l say what I need to say. I move with ease amid everything that moves. I wait peacefully with everything that waits. And I change in harmony with everything that changes. Maybe I've become one with the Great Oneness. But how would I know?"

Laughter

The Teaching:

In the moment between each moment when thoughts have forgotten the weight of their own burden, insight arises from its secret source and speaks as laughter. Without self or certainty, without reason or restraint, something unknowable puts together what has been taken apart. So the laughter that arises from deeper than thoughts can think is the sound of wholeness delighting in itself.

The Commentary:

"When I laugh," said Old Shu, "I laugh from the bottom of my belly, from deeper than thoughts can reach. A secret place opens inside me and the knowing that lives there roars its wisdom. Then the laughter thunders up and echoes into the world. I have silent laughter, too, the inward kind that only I can hear. And I also smile. But smiles aren't as deep as laughter because they still have some thoughts in them.

"Laughter is my language of thoughtless insight. When I laugh I stop thinking—like I'm between two thoughts. I enter the mystery of the Great Oneness, and I'm lost and found in its wholeness. Then, for just a moment, I have a clarity that's larger than myself, a wisdom that grabs me by the belly and shakes me to the bones. When I'm laughing I have no doubts, no questions, and there's just the Great Oneness mindlessly laughing at itself.

"Does this make any sense? Am I saying anything that means anything? Once, a travelling opera came to Ch'ang-an. A troupe of singers and dancers suddenly arrived from nowhere. They dressed in extravagant costumes, gathered in the village square, put on airs of passion and anger, and then they sang a drama of love and suffering, of revenge and death. All the while they banged on the skins of drums, blew on the wood of whistles and plucked on the strings of pipas. And then they left. And the world was exactly as before.

"What do I see when I look around me? I see people being born and dying. I see people forever filling with food and emptying of waste. I see people exhausting themselves with struggle and then reviving themselves with rest. I see people loving while others are hating, people crying while others are laughing—people everywhere, busily doing more things than my imagination can imagine. And everyone seems to be so seriously occupied—all engaged in a magnificent extravaganza, a tragical comedy or a comical tragedy that's countless times bigger than the opera at Ch'ang-an. Does anyone really know what they're doing? It's organized chaos! A huge joke!

"Now, when I see what I see, how can I take people seriously? Even though I eat and I breathe, even though I feel and I think, how can I take myself seriously? So I laugh—sometimes on the outside but mostly on the inside. That's all I can do, just laugh and watch my little self play its little part.

"Because I see what I see, I laugh. And because my little self plays in the world like everyone else, I laugh some more. But I can't just forget what I see and join in like everyone else. So I say what I say and I do what I do—but with a difference. That's why I laugh. And that's why I cry, too."

Learning

The Teaching:

Because things that are full cannot receive and things that are rigid cannot change, learning requires emptying and softening. So be open rather than closed. Be confused rather than certain. Discard answers to make room for questions. Then hold all questions gently so their asking does not disturb the searching. Since learning creates change, be ready for the unexpected. Stay calm. Be brave and resolute. The more that is learned, the less that is known. The less that is known, the greater the mystery. The greater the mystery, the smaller the self. And when self finally disappears into the mystery of everything, then the greatest of all teachings has been learned.

The Commentary:

"When I learn," said Old Shu, "I fill the emptiness that's within myself. If I can't find my emptiness, how can I learn?

"The first part of my learning was easy. I just filled with words and thoughts, with information and ideas, with opinions and arguments until my emptiness was full. When I seemed to have an answer to everything, my learning stopped because I lost my openness and my readiness. Then I became heavy and stiff, unable to change with everything's changing, unable to move in balance within the moving of the Great Oneness.

"The second part of my learning wasn't so easy. When I was full, I had to empty. And the more I filled, the more I had to empty. The greater my emptiness, the more I learned. And the more I learned, the more I had to empty. So, I learned to fill and empty at the same time. I remembered yet I forgot. Eventually, I held nothing to be true, nothing to be final, nothing to be certain. I became open and receptive, soft and receiving, confused and peaceful. Everything was surprising and new, endless and changing. I forgot myself. I forgot what I was doing and where I was going. Then, without a self or direction, I became — how can I say this—an emptiness that was filling, a simplicity that was receiving, a silence that was hearing, a stillness that was moving.

"For learning, I have three treasures that I keep: the first is stillness, the second is wonder, the third is trust.

"Stillness gives me inner balance, the unmoving centre that doesn't change with change, the silence that can't be broken by the noisy confusion of questions and answers. So, with stillness, I enter everything's changing. I become the place between opposites, the difference between thoughts. I learn without being disturbed and without causing disturbance. The passing seasons come and go, the struggling armies advance and retreat, birth and death follow each other, but I'm unmoved, unchanged—yet forever changed by all that happens.

"Wonder is curiosity honouring mystery. So everything I learn increases the measure of what I don't know, deepens my wonder and brings me closer to the mystery of the Great Oneness.

Finally, I trust learning and where it takes me. I trust the Great Oneness and the wisdom of its unfolding order. And so I trust that my filling will be an endless journey bringing me ever closer to the thoughtless thought at the very beginning of all thoughts.

"So I empty and I learn by entering the mystery of all the things I don't know. I learn and then I forget so the learning doesn't burden me. And somehow, this learning fills me with a knowing I can't explain, with a something I can only keep by forgetting what I've learned."

Losing

The Teaching:

Those who want too much will never have enough. Those with power must always be watchful. Earn reputation and fame, and then be forever burdened by the weight of importance. Keeping wastes effort and getting requires struggle. Riches can be stolen and wealth can be squandered. But losing finds what gaining cannot earn. Emptying achieves what filling cannot attain. The only treasure worth keeping is found at the end of losing. So empty and learn, discard and discover, release and find the balance between everything and nothing. Keep only what cannot be possessed and possess only what cannot be measured. Lose whatever can be gained to receive what is valued beyond value.

The Commentary:

"My life was simple when it began," said Old Shu, "then I made it complicated. When it finally became so complicated and confusing that I couldn't find who I was, I decided to give up what I'd become and return to where I started.

"On my path of losing, some things were taken away from me by the wisdom of life. Other things I gave away because they kept me from moving freely on the journey to my beginning. The more I doubted, the less I knew until my opinions became unimportant and my certainties seemed like passing dreams. The parts of myself that held me together began to fall away.

"The more I lost, the more I found. The lighter I became, the easier I moved. The less I understood, the more I saw. The less I knew, the larger grew the peaceful emptiness within me. Finally, I lost all the things I wasn't, fell into my own emptiness, and became a something that was a special nothing.

"Well, becoming nothing is a strange thing to become. But not any stranger than people who are always filling, who behave as if getting is everything, as if gaining and acquiring are the only important things worth doing? I came into life with nothing and I'll go out of life with nothing. And that must mean something.

"People who are always getting things seem to think that losing is like being defeated. But, for me, losing is a special kind of winning. Losing empties and prepares me for whatever's next. Whenever I lose, I become more open and receptive, more yielding and unbreakable. Losing softens my hardness, increases my strength, nurtures my humility, grows my compassion, brings me closer to the wisdom of the Great Oneness. Losing is an emptying that leads me to a special kind of filling."

Man

The Teaching:

Man is hardness of struggle. He is power of bone and strength of sinew. He is shaping and making, effort and intention. He is light in the mystery of darkness, the seeker of answers in the endless riddle of questions. He is movement and disquietude, a restless yearning that searches for relief in the vastness of the unknowable. Thus, all his struggles end in defeat, in poor little victories that are soon swept away by a wisdom greater than he can understand. So man comes to woman, seeking to find in her what he cannot find alone. And as his hard fullness is lost in her soft emptiness, he is momentarily comforted by forgetting. But this brief peace will not last until he becomes more than man, and learns that woman's dark mystery is the other part of his own wholeness.

The Commentary:

"When my body and mind would no longer be a boy," said Old Shu, "they became a man and I became what they wanted. So I challenged the world with my muscle and thought. I worked and I struggled. I asked questions and I found answers. I attacked life as if it were an enemy to be conquered. But no matter what I did, it was never enough. And I felt dissatisfied and incomplete.

"Why? Because I saw that my manhood was so small and that everything else was so big. I looked at the high mountains and the deep valleys, at the ancient stones and the endless sky, and I decided I could never overcome them all. Even my greatest effort seemed to accomplish little. When I tried to change the world, it resisted. And the more I tried, the more it resisted. Beneath every answer I found more questions. No matter what I did, I never came to the end of struggle.

"So I gave up trying to be a man. And then something incredible happened. When I softened, the world softened with

109

me. As I yielded to it, it yielded to me. If I moved with it, it moved with me—and then we moved together in harmony, like lovers in accord instead of enemies in opposition. By helping instead of forcing, everything I did became easier. When I didn't interfere, things seemed to do themselves. The less I struggled, the more I accomplished. But what I accomplished didn't seem to be the result of my effort so it didn't seem to belong to me.

"What finally happened? I lost some of the things that defined me as a man. I became something else—something less than a man or something more than a man, I don't know which. I still do the things a man does but now I move easily in the world, at peace with whatever happens. I think but I don't scheme. I work but I don't struggle. I act but I don't interfere. I enter the unfolding of things and I move with its moving. I wait patiently, allowing circumstances to find their own way. I have a will but it doesn't seem to be my own. I'm still me but I'm not me.

"Strange, isn't it, this thing I've become. I still look like a man but I've lost the inner form of a man. Whatever I am, people still recognize me as Old Shu. They call to me and I answer. But what they see is not really who I am. And what I know is not what most men know."

Mistakes

The Teaching:

All things rise and fall in the tumult of their order. Each thing appears and then disappears in its proper time. And the order unfolds without one mistake. So find the stillness that endures throughout the endless changing. Find the balance of the selfless centre that is undisturbed by whatever happens. From this quiet place comes the serenity of acceptance—for whatever is cannot be otherwise. Then thoughts clear, struggles end, judgments cease, and the rightness of each moment becomes apparent.

The Commentary:

"Like a man who is blind," said Old Shu, "I find my way by making mistakes. I bump into this and that. I meet obstructions here and there.
I trip on things. I stumble and fall.

"Whenever I encounter an obstacle—whenever things don't go smoothly—then I pause for a few moments, assess the situation and try something different. Sometimes I move in a new direction. Sometimes I just wait for circumstances to change. Then I begin again—and sometimes again and again—until a way opens for me. This is how I learn to move in the world.

"Slowly, without relying just on eyes to see, my other senses become more aware. I hear things that tell me where I am and what to avoid. Like my feet that recognize the slopes and textures of a familiar path, I learn to follow a narrow and winding course by staying between the roughness of its edges.

"As I go from place to place, I begin to feel and measure the emptiness in which I move. Each time I make a mistake, I learn something new and unexpected. Then my senses become sharper and more alert. The wholeness of my body begins to feel the difference between places that are welcoming and those that are not. This is how I find openings and opportunities, places of grace where I can move without meeting resistance or creating disturbance. Each mistake guides me to where I will be received.

"Who has eyes to see in the darkness of the unknowable? Who has ears to hear the teachings of utter silence? Who has thoughts to know the wisdom of the Great Oneness? Who can find the secret way, the hidden and unseen opening that lies between the apparent forms of everything?

"So I find what isn't by attending to what is. I pay close attention to where I am. I hone my senses to their sharpest clarity. And then I make mistakes.

"Every time I make a mistake, I return to my humility. I remember the balance that I keep deep inside. Then I find the inner stillness where I'm empty and trusting and open, where I meet each new moment with an innocent freshness. And then the mistake does not belong to me.

"Each mistake teaches me something I can't learn any other way. Slowly I begin to sense how things happen. I come closer to the wisdom of the Great Oneness, to my belonging in its wholeness, and to the course of the winding path that unfolds beneath my feet.

"And that's how I find my way. I learn by going where I cannot go. I learn by doing what I cannot do."

Mystery

The Teaching:

Without one question, without one answer, without one word of explanation, each thing becomes just what it is. When each thing is just what it is, where is the mystery? The mystery is created by questions that have no answers and by answers that invite more questions. Without one question or answer—without even one moment's pause—all mystery disappears.

The Commentary:

"I don't understand," said Old Shu. "And I don't understand why I don't understand. I don't understand my own thoughts and I don't understand why they can't understand themselves. I don't know anything. And all I know is that I don't know.

"I look at my seeing and I listen to my hearing but they're mysteries. I don't understand this seeing that I'm seeing or this hearing that I'm hearing. I don't understand the green of fresh grasses on spring meadows or the splashing of mountain streams on wet rocks. I don't understand stones or leaves or sky. And I don't understand that I don't understand.

"The Great Oneness seems to move and change. Something vast and formless seems to unfold into form and order but I don't understand how this happens. Somehow wholeness becomes whole and all its myriad parts remember their belonging.

"I think about my thinking and it's a mystery. I listen to my words and they become strange noises. I don't understand the silence between my words. And I don't understand the emptiness between my thoughts.

"My thoughts reach inward and outward as far as they can reach but they can't find answers. My head spins. My heart pounds. My belly tightens with uncertainty. I'm lost and dismayed in a huge confusion. Small and bewildered, I'm too overwhelmed to struggle. So I surrender to the unknowable and I sink into a boundless nothing. Then, thoughtlessly, I enter the emptiness between everything I can think.

"Suddenly—as if by magic—something happens without happening, something is understood without understanding. Searching vanishes. Questions fall away. Doubts disappear. Everything is clear and simple. And the Old Shu, who once was me, becomes peacefully quiet. Winds blow through his formless bones. Streams flow in his endless veins. Sunlight warms his invisible flesh. Then—whatever he does, however he comes or goes, whether he moves or waits—he's as serene and timeless as an ancient stone in a silent field. He's calmly full and wonderfully empty, contentedly amazed and brilliantly alive in a oneness that just is.

"Doesn't anyone else understand without questions? Doesn't anyone else know without answers? Doesn't anyone else disappear into the mystery of everything—and then have the mystery disappear?"

Oneness

The Teaching:

Something unsayable resides in the nameless place between differences. Like a hidden stillness that is nowhere and everywhere, it binds each thing to every other thing, collecting separateness into togetherness and eliminating all distinctions. To know this oneness, mend and bend all the broken words of straight thoughts into a full roundness. Beyond the heavy weight of words and the small shape of thoughts, listen to a greater call. Oneness begins as no sound, no thought, no disturbance in the still balance of all differences. Hear it when words are unspoken and silence speaks. Find it when mind is still and thoughts are thoughtless. Then, without a single question or thought, a thunderous silence whispers the wordless teaching.

The Commentary:

"From high on Mount Shan," said Old Shu, "I can see the faraway hills and valleys tumbling into the distance, their shadowed forms finally disappearing beyond the reach of my seeing. So I look at my seeing, I welcome what it sees, and I embrace everything that's beyond it.

"My thoughts follow my seeing, stretching beyond the reach of my understanding, tumbling into the distance beyond what I know. Over this edge of understanding, things are not what they're called and words no longer have meaning.

"To reach this place beyond words and meaning, I send my thoughts beyond the limit of themselves, falling and curving to encircle a greatness that's more than I can think. I enter a formless shape and a shapeless form, a something that's nothing and a nothing that's something. Then I see what I can't see and I know what I can't know. My silence fills with the fullness of all that is. My pounding heart drums with excitement and I'm overcome by the welcome of belonging, like a long-lost traveller returning to a remembered home.

115

"I'm on a mountain. I call myself Old Shu and I say I'm a hunchback. I use different words to speak of differences but I recognize only oneness. I walk from place to place but I go nowhere. I feel small and I feel large. I'm all things but I'm nothing. I'm empty but I'm filled with wonder. The wonder overflows the thing I call myself, courses through the distant valleys and over the disappearing hills. It stirs the churning clouds with rain and feeds the nourishing rivers. It gathers the white moon into a blanket of light. It ignites the warming sun. The white flakes of winter snow become the coloured flowers of wild meadows. The high stars of night skies become the living trees of deep forests. Then silence speaks to me. And what I now know, I can never say.

"When I come down from Mount Shan and return to Ch'ang-an, I'm peaceful and easy with everything that happens. I walk the cobblestone streets with my nose close to the dusty ground but I see only the oneness of everything that is. The air teems with the busy sounds of the village—with the shouts of playing children, with braying donkeys and crowing roosters—but I hear only the singing of a great harmony.

"My seeing eyes well with tears. My beating heart throbs with a contented aching. And I don't know whether to laugh or cry.

"Strange that I should feel so full and empty, more awake than being awake, so grateful for something I don't even understand."

Opposites

The Teaching:

Opposites are the creation of each other, the invention of ordinary thinking. So, without opposites, find another kind of understanding. Open to the place that is neither here nor there, neither this nor that, neither self nor other. Between opposites, all differences fall away and all distinctions disappear. Then a clarity of seeing is seen, a fullness of hearing is heard, and each thing becomes the wonder of itself. Even the smallest and the lowest become great beyond saying. Therefore, these are the teachings: opposites create the place between opposites; from the place between opposites comes the place between thoughts; from the place between thoughts comes insight. This is why opposites are called the very beginning of deepest awareness.

The Commentary:

"I have two feet for walking," said Old Shu, "but my balance is in the nameless centre that's neither left nor right. I have arms and legs, bones and breath, thoughts and feelings, but my wholeness is somewhere else — in a place that has no words.

"A mountain is called a mountain and a valley is called a valley so that makes one thing and another. The mountain is above and the valley is below — now there's up and down. The valley has a river — so now there's land and water, dry and wet. The river runs into a distant sea — so now there's movement and stillness, near and far, here and there. But there's something else that's neither one thing nor another.

"Because of one thing, I can find another. Because of what is, I can find what isn't. Because of opposites, I can find the place between opposites. Between everything that is, there's something else, something that's not immediately apparent. Because of the fullness of what is, I can find the emptiness of what's not. Because of what's ordinary, I can find what's not ordinary.

117

"Why do people lose their way in the ordinary affairs of life? Because they think they can choose one thing without another. Because they expect they can have up without down, good without bad, joy without sorrow, success without failure, beginnings without endings. They don't seem to understand that the Great Oneness is whole, that each thing always comes with something else. If they'd remember this, they'd think big enough to keep their balance. Then they'd be ready for whatever happens.

"To be ready for whatever happens, I think big enough for everything and small enough for nothing. I think in opposites to find_what's between opposites. By searching between what is, I find what isn't.

"So I become fullness and emptiness. I'm myself and not myself. Poised between opposites, opposites disappear. Outside and inside become each other, everything and nothing are the same. And from this place, I become more than myself — a living wholeness, a moving stillness, a readiness balanced in each unfolding moment."

Order

The Teaching:

Order creates order by the great unfolding of itself. Beginnings and endings arise from each other. Night follows day, rest follows effort and death follows birth. Everything rises and falls, coming and going in the rhythm of its own breathing. Therefore, know joy by sorrow and pleasure by suffering. Recognize death as birth's other blessing. Accept the inevitable and welcome the natural. Since each small moment fulfils what is both great and simple, everything that happens is honoured for its wisdom. Trust the wisdom of order. Move within its moving. Follow the outer by attending to the inner. When discipline is resolute enough to be freedom and attention is unwavering enough to be forgotten, then the unfolding course of order is apparent and all things will happen in their proper time.

The Commentary:

"In my ordinary life," said Old Shu, "I never talk or think about order. Things just are as they are. Things just happen as they happen. So I move easily and thoughtlessly with the Great Oneness, following the grace of its unfolding.

"How do I follow the grace of its unfolding? By being careful not to believe in words—and by not thinking too much. If I start thinking about order, I have to think about disorder, too. Suddenly, as if by magic, there are differences everywhere. Then the simplicity of things is lost—and that's the beginning of confusion and the end of grace.

"So I take care not to disturb the simplicity of things. Just one mention of order and it's already too late to stop the confusion. This is the trouble with words, with teachings, and with the endless exercises of fancy thinking. All their definitions and explanations disturb the quiet simplicity that's needed to follow an order that's formless, that always escapes the shape of words and thoughts.

119

"So I walk a narrow path between differences. People who see me wandering through the Wu Valley see the outer form of me but they don't see the formless me. And they don't understand my wayward way.

"On this path that I travel, the world changes but stays the same. I don't know how this happens. I just know that for me there's a stillness that changes and a changing that's still—a discipline that allows me to be still and a freedom that allows me to move. So I release into a middle place between these differences, into something empty and formless in which all differences disappear.

"To do this, I need the inner discipline to soften and release, to let the stillness become its own changing. And when I become aimless and lost, I move with a grace and a timing that always takes me where I'm supposed to be. And where am I supposed to be? Just wherever I am.

"People who notice what I do and where I go think I'm just confused and lost. That's because they don't see the nameless order in which I move. I don't follow their plans or intentions—I don't even follow my own. Instead, I move softly with the unfolding course of endless moments, following the wisdom of the unplanned and the unintended. I come and I go. I arrive and I leave. Things change but somehow stay the same. I move but I'm still, always peaceful and balanced, easy and calm, unhurried and timeless amid everything's passing."

Ordinary

The Teaching:

Greatness is never great. Simplicity is never simple. The ordinary is never ordinary. Those who do not see the extraordinary in the ordinary are not seeing. So be as innocent and amazed as a newborn child. Without the burden of self or differences, and without the weight of understanding or judgment, find the extraordinary in the ordinary. Attend to the fullness of each moment until the present is wholly present and the ordinary is no longer ordinary. When the extraordinary finally returns to ordinary, then everything will be the same again — but different.

The Commentary:

"I sleep and then I awake," said Old Shu. "I breathe and I walk. I see and I hear. I think and I feel. The heat of summer warms my flesh and the cold of winter chills my bones. The silence of the sun brightens each day. The pines at the Tien-po Temple grow upward into the sky. The emptiness in the Wu Valley receives the Han River. The stillness of Mount Shan silently waits as time slowly passes.

"Isn't the ordinary extraordinary enough? When I see with my seeing, I'm overcome by whatever I see. When I feel with my feeling, I'm overcome by whatever I feel. I think with my thinking and I'm overcome by whatever I think. When I can't even arrive at the simplest answer without getting lost in countless questions — when I can't even explain how I fall asleep — shouldn't I be amazed by what's ordinary?

"My eyes fill with the miracle of seeing. My skin tingles with the delight of touching. The autumn leaves talk to me and the spring winds sing to me. My five senses flood with awareness and my thoughts think the magic of themselves. So, does it really matter where I am or what I do? I think, I feel, I'm alive — lost in the wonder of merely being.

121

"Emperor Yao has hoards of gold stored in secret places, locked in vaults, hidden safely in the darkness of holes and caves. Because his gold doesn't tarnish, he thinks it's special and that he can keep it forever. If he looked beyond the walls of his palace to the mountain meadows, he'd see the wild lilies coming and going in the freedom of their seasons. Without his approval or disapproval, without his laws or decrees, the bending grasses dance to the caress of wind. The fragrances of pine and sandalwood waft unhindered through the forest air. What is the smell of gold? Does it glisten in the darkness? Does it whisper like bending grasses in passing breezes?

"Give me the air and the light of each ordinary day. Give me fields and meadows, grasses and trees, mountains and streams. Emperor Yao can have his gold. The ordinary is enough for me."

Patience

The Teaching:

A waiting stillness fills the nameless place between passing and becoming. Purpose ends and self disappears into the vastness of the present. Then each breath of thought takes an endless moment to notice all that happens. Who waits when self is lost in time, when purpose lets go of each passing moment, when patience fills with forever? Patience is the beginning of a softness that allows timing to find its own time, that allows becoming to become itself, that allows each thing to discover its proper place in the unfolding wholeness.

The Commentary:

"As for patience," said Old Shu, "I begin with forever, I end with forever, and I keep forever in the centre of each moment.

"What do I mean? I mean that I follow the wisdom of nature and I learn from the course of its timelessness. I open to where I am and I lose myself in that moment. Then I behave as if I'm everywhere and nowhere, as if I'm someone and no one, as if I care and don't care.

"Does this make any sense? What I'm trying to say is difficult for words to say so I'll try to say it with other words.

"The day waits in the night until the sun rises of itself. Then the night waits in the day until the sun sets of itself. Day and night don't hurry. Each follows the pace of the other and each arrives in its proper time.

"When day becomes day and night becomes night, nothing can force them to become what they're not. Since nothing can change what arrives in its own time, I enter the natural course of things and I follow its unfolding wisdom.

"So I wait patiently and I follow the order of the Great

Oneness. I don't hurry or challenge the course of things. I enter the centre of forever and I take the time that's required to do things carefully, to attend to the rightness of each moment's becoming. And when I act, my doing arises spontaneously from somewhere that doesn't belong to me. Then I'm clear and decisive, without an instant of doubt or restraint.

"My life is filled with the fullness between birth and death. But no matter how quickly or slowly I go, I can't make it shorter or longer. So I enter the centre of each moment—the place where time is not important—and I move patiently within its unfolding."

Perfection

The Teaching:

Search in the present to find perfection. Receive each moment exactly as it is. When each moment is accepted for its own fullness, it becomes only itself. Then all differences fall away and a stillness replaces the passing of all things. In the fullness of this present, silence speaks and explains without words. Deaf ears listen and hear. Blind eyes open and see. And such still moments become so full, who would trade one time for any other time, one place for any other place, the fullness of each moment for any other moment?

The Commentary:

"Sometimes my rice bowl is full," said Old Shu, "and sometimes it's empty. Sometimes laughter bursts from my belly and sometimes tears fall from my eyes. When whatever happens is just what happens, how can it be otherwise? When everything is just as it is, what's the difference between one thing and another?

"When I'm wholly present—when I'm just where I am—everything is just as it is. And that's that. When everything's so simple, why make it complicated? But people want more of things. So they decide what each moment should or shouldn't be. They invent good and bad, better or worse. And then they dream of what's best.

"People get lost in such big thoughts. Then they forget where they are and they think too small. And how do they do this? They place their little selves in the very centre of the Great Oneness and then they expect its wisdom to serve only them—to neglect everything else, to grant only their wishes, to flood them with all the blessings of Heaven and Earth.

"The farmers of the Wu Valley went to the Tien-po Temple to pray for rain. They did all the proper things—made

125

offerings, burned incense, beat drums—but they forgot to think big enough. When the clouds opened and the deluge came, it quenched their thirst and watered their fields. But it also overflowed the Han River, covered their land, and washed away their crops and houses. A good thing, they learned, is only a little of a good thing.

"So I think big enough to think small. When I'm hot, I see a garden snake basking contentedly on sunny stones. When I'm thirsty, I watch a cricket drinking its fill from a crystal dewdrop. When I'm cold, I remember the autumn seeds resting quietly under the winter snow. Why should I disturb their contentment with prayers of my own?

"So I become more than myself. And when I'm at peace with the wisdom of the Great Oneness, I find perfection everywhere."

Power

The Teaching:

Forget intention. Abandon purpose. Surrender willfulness. Find the direction that is without direction. Choose the course that neither controls nor submits. Move with the wholeness of things. Become the wisdom and wonder of an unseen order becoming itself. Here is the very centre of power, the selfless place that creates no disturbance at all.

The Commentary:

"The downward flow of rivers cannot be stopped," said Old Shu. "The arrival of mornings will not wait. The spring grasses grow without the decrees of Emperor Yao. And all the potions and elixirs in his imperial apothecaries cannot stop the coming of death. So, do people really think they have power?

"If I had power, what would I do with it? Change the world? Improve it? Better myself? I don't think so. Those with power simply disturb the natural order of things and cause trouble.

"I have no influence yet I'm contented. I have no power yet I'm at peace with the world. Although I'm small and I'm insignificant, although I don't try and I don't struggle, the world moves in harmony with me. Does this seem impossible? I'll try to explain.

"Because I know myself, I become who I am—growing quietly out of my own centre like a plant from a seed. By attending to my own nature, I move in accord with myself. By being in accord with myself, I follow the unfolding order of each moment. Because I'm wholly present—attuned to exactly where I am—I'm in harmony with whatever happens. Thus, when I know myself, I'm able to find my place in the wholeness of things.

"And how do I find my place in the wholeness of things?

By not having selfish interests and by not being purposeful, I see what is. By not thinking and by not deliberating, I don't doubt and I don't hesitate. Then I can respond directly to the clarity of each unfolding moment. So I enter the order of these moments and I move with their wholeness. By attending to the order of what is, and by moving with the unfolding of each moment, my judgment becomes flawless and my timing impeccable.

"But my judgment and my timing are not my own. Because they're not mine, I have no power. Although I've become one with the Great Oneness and I've entered its wisdom, I'm like an innocent child who's lost and confused within the wonder of a vast mystery.

"Because I don't know, I'm open. Because I'm open, I receive. Because I receive, I discover. Because I discover, I know. And what do I know? Nothing. I'm empty. Instead of being Old Shu, I'm readiness poised on the edge of whatever's happening, thoughtlessly entering the Great Oneness moment by moment. Thus, I become one with its wisdom and its power. I know nothing yet I move with certainty. I control nothing yet I wait with trust.

"To acquire wisdom and power, I don't struggle and I don't resist. I just go where I go and do what I do. Therefore, I'm found by the Great Oneness and I become one with its unfolding. Lost in its vastness, I become nothing and everything, a special emptiness moving in a boundless grace."

Questions

The Teaching:

Questions are invented by words and their answers are given by words, so the only answers to questions are more words and then more questions. Answers will never satisfy all the questions that words can invent. Ask one question and more will follow until the sound of the unspoken answer cannot be heard. Before each question is asked, its answer is already known. Hidden within an inner waiting is the silence of deep remembering. Before thoughts can be thought and words can be formed, a secret answer whispers from a forgotten clarity. To answer questions before they arise, listen without questions.

The Commentary:

"Questions," said Old Shu, "are always bigger than answers. So I live in questions. And whenever I ask questions, I ask them without expecting answers.

"Questions without answers are a way of staying undivided and whole. Because questions can never be finally answered, I follow them to the boundless place where they arise, then I enter their beginning. Entering questions before they have been asked is like living the mystery of the Great Oneness.

"Now I've just said something about questions that seems like an answer. Maybe I should just be quiet and let the Great Oneness speak for itself. But I have some other things to say, so I might as well say them.

"Just because questions can be asked, doesn't mean they have answers. Some questions are the shape of answers. Some questions are the shape of the people who ask them. But all questions are the shape of words. So I use questions but I don't trust them.

"Do I contradict myself? I live in questions but I don't

expect the comfort of answers. And I don't expect to reach the end of questions. Anyone who starts with a question will never finish with an answer.

"People who are foolish enough to take questions seriously can entertain themselves for a lifetime. Each question will have an answer and then each answer will have another question. So searching for answers is the same as searching for questions. That's why I don't take questions seriously. And that's why I leave the wholeness of things undisturbed—so the questions can ask me.

"When the questions are asking me, I become the questions—I enter the asking and I empty of all certainty. When the questions that are asking me become bigger than the questions I can ask, the answers that are answering me become bigger than the answers I can understand. Then I'm carried into a wholeness that lives and a silence that speaks, into an emptiness that's full and a stillness that moves. I become peaceful and easy, like I've entered the wisdom of the Great Oneness. And then I fill with an unspoken knowing—with an answer that's like a question."

Readiness

The Teaching:

Readiness waits in the timeless centre of each moment's becoming. Therefore, stay wholly present. Be attentive and alert. Balance on the edge of each moment's fullness and become the living readiness of everything's unfolding. Since readiness is balance meeting the arrival of whatever comes, be relaxed yet disciplined, flexible yet firm, cautious yet fearless. Avoid the certainty that cannot respond to surprise and the uncertainty that cannot recognize opportunity. In the practice of readiness, remember that openings can occur quickly, that easiness can suddenly become difficult, that even formidable opposition can reveal weakness. Changing circumstances favour those with a patient readiness.

The Commentary:

"Because I expect nothing," said Old Shu, "I'm always ready. Because I'm certain of nothing, I'm empty and open. When I don't think or doubt, I meet whatever happens without hesitation. With nothing to confuse me, I act with decisive clarity. With nothing to hinder me, I act with a timing that fits each situation. This is my lightness meeting the unfolding grace of the Great Oneness.

"I also have an inner discipline that's always ready because it expects anything. It's the strength that bends but doesn't break, the yielding that changes but keeps its essence, the course that wanders but never loses its direction. This is my heaviness meeting the unfolding grace of the Great Oneness.

"So I'm as light as blowing thistledown and I'm as heavy as mighty mountains. I respond to the smallest whim of breezes but I'm unmoved by the roaring blast of storms.

"Because of this lightness and heaviness, I follow what I can't explain and I become what I don't understand. I'm at one

131

with the wholeness of things but I'm separate and different. I'm at ease with everything's unfolding but I'm tempered with the strength of discipline. I have a mind but no mind of my own. From the precipice of each moment, I plunge to my death and rebirth so I'm always at the last and the first of my life. I act with abandon. I wait without care. Although I never anticipate, I'm never surprised.

"I prepare myself from head to toe, from inside to outside, from beginning to end. Therefore, I'm young but I'm old, I'm innocent but I'm experienced, I'm lost but I'm ready. Because I'm everything and I'm nothing, I move in the grace of each moment. My lightness lifts me to the promises of Heaven and my heaviness lowers me to the blessings of Earth. A nameless form holds me in its order. The Great Oneness carries me in its embrace. And I'm at peace with all that I do."

Seeing

The Teaching:

With thoughts as still as stone and with eyes as open as sky, look from the very centre of seeing. Without question or doubts, without explanations or answers, welcome the nameless sensations that appear. To see with more than eyes can see, simply open eyes and see. When seeing is seeing itself, a silent brilliance illuminates the empty eyes, brightens the night within and shines deeper than understanding can reach. Then awareness fills with wordless wonder, the vibrant air tingles and shimmers in a living light, and each moment is more vivid than amazement.

The Commentary:

"When I see," said Old Shu, "I just see what I see. From high on Mount Shan, I can see the Han River, the village of Ch'ang-an, and the hills and valleys disappearing beyond. I seem to be here and they seem to be there.

"But I also see the seeing. Between where I am and what I see, there's a place that's neither here nor there. And when I forget who I am and what I'm called—when I forget my body and myself—then I see the place between here and there, the something which connects this with that and makes seeing more than seeing.

"When I see, I see with this seeing. Then I see clearly. But I don't see shapes and forms to recognize and call by name. I don't even think river or village, hills or valleys. I have no words for anything. My seeing isn't bound by the shape of answers or explanations, by the limits of my thoughts or myself. The seeing just is—somewhere but nowhere— fresh and alive, unchanged and unburdened with ideas or judgments.

"Everything in this seeing is vivid and vital, but none of the things I see have any meaning. Because they have no meaning,

133

each thing is free to be itself. Without my thoughts to make them less than they are, each thing becomes more than I can understand. And when I lose myself in the seeing—in the place between here and there—there's no me, either. Then, no river, no village, no hills or valleys. Nothing. And so, everything.

"Sometimes, when I try to say something that's more than words can say, I come close to the edge of nonsense. And then I don't know if I've said anything or not. Maybe it would be better if I just said, 'Look with your bones! See with your belly!' But who would understand that?"

Self

The Teaching:

As self becomes larger, everything else becomes smaller until belonging is lost. As self becomes certain, everything else becomes uncertain until wisdom is forgotten. Without belonging and wisdom, thinking becomes confused and doing becomes undisciplined. Then crisis follows. To avoid misfortune, balance self and other. Find the place where they are the same yet different, separate yet not separate. When inner and outer become each other, then self finds its proper place in the wholeness of things, and belonging and wisdom are restored.

The Commentary:

"In the tumult and noise of market day," said Old Shu, "the fruit is piled high in the stalls of the farmers. But the flesh of each fruit is silent within the cover of its skin. And the essence of each fruit is silent within the darkness of its seed. So for a long time I was lost because I was listening to outer voices rather than inner ones, because I couldn't hear what was speaking within me.

"At the death of my little self—when I became quiet and still inside—all my words ended, all my thoughts stopped, and all the outer voices were finally silent. Then I was alone with the empty remains of who I used to be.

"That's when I began to hear unspoken voices. These voices didn't speak with words, they spoke with silence—nameless urges that began to guide me here or there, that made effortless choices and found the proper timing for whatever I did. Then I realized my emptiness was full of something I'd never noticed before. And when I listened carefully, I could hear instructions that came as secret hints and hushed callings, less than whispers that arose from somewhere deeper than bones and led me to places that only I could go.

"Where was I going? Where was I being taken? When I

135

followed what I felt instead of what I thought, it seemed like I was being led along a path I'd travelled before. I couldn't remember the destination but the direction was familiar, comfortable and welcoming. When I was on this path, I was peaceful and contented, in balance with everything that was happening.

"Careful listening eventually taught me that my belly knew how to hear these wordless voices, how to follow these inner urges. But sometimes, when I'm inattentive, I get off this path and I feel lost and confused. Then, wherever I try to go, I feel like I'm struggling uphill, moving against myself.

"Whenever this happens, I stop and I wait. And when I've become inwardly still, I listen until I feel an urge arising out of the quiet depth of myself. When this urge comes, I just follow it and then, suddenly and effortlessly, I'm back on my path again.

"Now, I rarely get lost. I still don't know where I'm going. But I know the path is mine. And whenever I'm on it, I feel like I'm at home—like I'm becoming myself."

Silence

The Teaching:

Silence sounds in the stillness between differences. The deepest wisdom echoes between each word. The greatest understanding resides between each thought. Therefore, hear what words cannot say to know what thoughts cannot think. Listen between words to hear their formless wisdom. Deep-listen and enter the clarity of silence. Deep-speak and pronounce the wonders of the unsayable. Answer without words. Hear without ears. Understand without thoughts. Become the formless silence that arises from the very centre of knowing.

The Commentary:

"When people are speaking to me," said Old Shu, "I listen to the silence between their words and I hear what they don't say. When I'm speaking to them, I listen to the silence between my own words and I hear what I can't say.

"To meet the silence of what I can't say, I climb to the top of Mount Shan and I lose myself in the vastness of stone and sky. Then I listen to something that's more than my words can say, and I learn something that's more than my thoughts can think.

"Maybe no one thinks about silence. Maybe no one understands what I'm trying to say. Maybe my words sound foolish—empty and hollow, trivial and silly in the immensity of things. Maybe my thoughts seem confused—small and lost, futile and useless in the vastness of things. Maybe everything I say or think is of no importance.

"Doesn't anyone else have this feeling? Doesn't anyone else recognize this in themselves? Isn't anyone else overcome by wonder and amazement, left foolish and confused by the mystery of everything? That's when my voice becomes quiet and my thoughts become still, when I begin to hear what I can't say and I begin to know what I can't think.

"When I'm peacefully alone on the mountain—quiet and still in the mystery that holds me—I become one with the air and the light, with the mists and the clouds. And without a sound I hear the bright sun singing its crystal clarity, the ancient stone whispering its patient wisdom, the timeless sky shouting its unspoken certainty. And without a sound or a self, I become the vast emptiness that holds all things, that connects all things, that is all things. My thoughts empty and my emptiness fills with a wordless silence. I become generations passing and being born, forests arising and returning to dust. Like gentle rain becoming ageless rivers and seas, I become everything and nothing, an endless stillness listening to the silence of itself.

"So I go to Mount Shan to be alone. And when I lose myself there, I find a place between places, a place between my own words and thoughts, a special silence that knows what I don't know."

Simplicity

The Teaching:

When simplicity becomes complicated, its wisdom is hidden. When the ordinary is adorned and decorated, its value is obscured. Therefore, honour the simple and the ordinary. Remember beginnings. Return to the primal way and follow its unfolding grace. When simplicity is undisturbed, accord finds itself, order maintains itself, balance keeps itself, and all the parts of wholeness move in concert with each other. Then, without struggle or effort, a course opens through adversity and danger.

The Commentary:

"When I forget the simplicity of things," said Old Shu, "and I attend to the complexity of things, I get lost and confused. It's simplicity that gives me my direction and patience, my balance and peacefulness.

"The Han River flows by the village of Ch'ang-an on its way to the sea. When the wind blows against its current, the water becomes rough and dangerous. Then all the fishermen are alert and careful because their boats could swamp and sink. No one can see beneath the waves and into the depth of the river. But below its restless surface, the water always moves downward, unaffected by the disturbance and the turmoil above.

"Beneath the complexity of things, there's a deep simplicity that never varies from its own course. The surface may appear complex and strange but the depth below is primal and unchanging. So, I move with the current that's below me, with the downward wisdom that carries me where it will. And by keeping its course beneath whatever I do, I keep my balance and my direction.

"What do I need to live? Some rice, some rain and a few rags of clothing. What do I need to be happy? Ordinary thoughts

139

that are free and unburdened by care. What do I need for comfort? The warmth of the daily sun and the quiet of the nightly dark. Everything else is just unnecessary complexity.

"When Emperor Yao decided to build his palace, he summoned experts from near and far to determine where the walls and rooms should be placed, where the windows and doors belonged, and what the colours and textures should be so that all the parts were in harmony with each other. And when he decided to decorate his palace with silks and treasures, he fussed and fretted where each piece should go for fear of losing a hundredth measure of beauty. Then, when he wasn't distracted by his palace, he had his affairs of state to conduct—intricate and complex manoeuvres of force and diplomacy that occupied his days and nights with worries and intrigues.

"As for me, I prefer simplicity, the uncomplicated and the ordinary. The beauty of my palace is the valleys and fields and mountains of each day. My floor is the soil and rock of the land. My ceiling is the clouds and winds of the sky. My walls and doors and windows are the vast expanse of the four directions. Unlike Emperor Yao, I don't trouble myself with luxury and wealth, with plots and strategies, with endless power struggles just so I can stay where I am. I prefer to drift with the current of the river. Its simple wisdom always takes me where I'm going."

Solitude

The Teaching:

All the confusion and turmoil of change swirls and churns around a nameless centre. But the centre itself is peaceful and still, quiet and unmoved. Solitude finds the inner amid the outer, separates the nameless from the named, remembers the secret balance that welcomes all the wonders of awareness. Birth begins what death ends; solitude finds what distractions hide. When self is replaced with the unnamed and the unthought, all the myriad differences return to their oneness and solitude fills to overflowing.

The Commentary:

"Solitude nourishes me," said Old Shu. "It sharpens my senses, deepens my insight, strengthens my balance and increases my power. I've learned to find solitude anywhere but I find it more easily on Mount Shan.

"From high on this mountain, the village of Ch'ang-an becomes a patch of quiet order where little people live in little houses and move silently along little streets. The Han River draws itself like a dark brushstroke through the living green of the Wu Valley. And beyond the farmers' fields and orchards, the gentle blue of far-off hills rise and fall into a distance beyond seeing. A scent of cool pines freshens the bright air that I breathe. A blanket of soft mosses spreads its slow patience over the ageless stones where I stand. Ancient trees keep me company. And in such a place as this, I learn more than ordinary teaching can teach me.

"Even though I walk the steep mountain paths, I'm as still as sky. Even though the wind pierces the rough weave of my cloak, I'm contented and undisturbed, peaceful and serene. The Great Oneness nourishes me, embraces me and guides me along a course of grace.

"How can I use words to say what happens in this grace?

141

I disappear into soundless sound and timeless time. I enter the beauty of passing and becoming. Without a separate body—without even separate thoughts—I become a formless form moving within the order of a vast unfolding. Wholly empty, I enter the wisdom of becoming. Then my emptiness fills with a gentle fullness. And this mere bag of dust, with the name of Old Shu, becomes one with the Great Oneness.

"That's when I can't even speak my own words. I can't even think my own thoughts. I don't know who I am. There's no Old Shu. He's gone, lost in something bigger than himself. So I walk as if I'm not walking. I breathe as if I'm not breathing. My eyes see the wonder of seeing and my ears hear the wonder of hearing. The wind speaks a language I remember in my bones.

"I enter the harmony of moving and changing, the order of countless patterns and rhythms, the peace of a nameless design. I can't describe the beauty of the wholeness that carries me beyond my little self. I'm empty and yet I overflow with the magic of everything that is. The brilliance of each moment overcomes me. I know something—something that I can't understand. Then my eyes fill with tears and my body wants to cry with the joy of being nothing and everything, of being at home in the embrace of the Great Oneness.

"When I come down from the solitude of Mount Shan and return to the village and the valley, I carry deep inside myself the quiet and the stillness that nourishes and guides me."

Spontaneity

The Teaching:

Pause just an instant and the moment has already passed. In the rush of everything's changing, planning is no longer an option. Deliberation is too slow. Thinking takes too long. To be the spontaneity that finds perfect timing, be both alert and thoughtless, both reckless and disciplined. Enter the fullness of the present, become one with its unfolding wholeness, and then move with each moment's urging.

The Commentary:

"Spontaneity," said Old Shu, "is myself being itself. When I release to my inner nature, I enter the freedom of who I am. Then my thinking and my doing arise from the nameless place that's their own home. And the separate parts of myself are comfortable and peaceful with each other, as if they belong together.

"When this wholeness is itself—when it's unbothered and unaffected by things that don't belong to it—then my spontaneity is undivided and pure. That's when the differences within me disappear and I move with an ease and a grace that's effortless.

"I have two feet. And ever since they were born, they've wanted to walk and run, to move as they like, to be free and spontaneous. The less I meddle, the better they work. When I don't disturb them with instructions, they don't get confused. When I allow them to take their own steps, they behave flawlessly. So we have an understanding. I let them do what they like and they agree to stay under me. That's why I never stumble or fall. If I don't interfere, they're always fast and nimble, sure and reliable, always ready for what they're supposed to do.

"If Emperor Yao would respect the wisdom of his people like I respect the wisdom of my feet, he could govern his country easily, his subjects would be more contented, and everything would work better. Too many rules and regulations just create trouble.

"The courtiers in Emperor Yao's imperial retinue have to agree with his every taste and judgment. Once they've surrendered to his approval or disapproval and given up who they are, then they've lost their own spirit and they become the poorest form of themselves. When the people of a country have to conform to its traditions and rituals, when they have to honour the sayings and teachings of its patriarchs, then they lose their own way. And without their own way, their vitality grows stiff and suffers, and everyone is poorer.

"For people to be fulfilled, they have to follow the wisdom that arises from within their own nature. If this doesn't happen, they become lost and confused, bent and twisted into a shape that nobody likes. Then chaos threatens.

"So the art of governing allows people to find their own way. Give them too many instructions, impose too many regulations, and they won't even be able to walk. Without spontaneity, people can't become themselves and a country can't be alive and strong.

"Like a living self, a country needs a head—Emperor Yao will do. Let him assign duties to his people. Let him expect obedience and loyalty. Then, let him stand aside so they can take their own steps. Thus, without any effort from him, they'll grow his food, fight his enemies, build his canals, service his roads, and pay his taxes. But they'll also attend to their own needs, maintain their vitality, create a strong country, fulfil themselves, and be contented. And all this is done when people live their own spontaneity."

Stillness

The Teaching:

Something within all changing does not change. Something within all differences is not different. In the very centre of everything's becoming, there is a stillness from which becoming arises. Everything moves from stillness and returns to stillness. So, from beginnings to endings, stillness is always present. Although it is intangible, it can be discerned. Although it is hidden, it can be found. Therefore, forget ambition and progress. Abandon ceremony and propriety. Renounce judgment and opinion. Without attachment to differences, without the distractions of direction or purpose, empty and enter the unchanging and the boundless. Then move with an inner stillness and follow the way of wholeness. Proper doing arises from stillness. Perfect balance depends on stillness. And stillness is the source of deepest peace.

The Commentary:

"The water of a river moves," said Old Shu, "but the river itself doesn't move. Winds blow but the empty sky is clear and unchanged. The sun rises and sets, the moon waxes and wanes, the seasons come and go but everything remains the same. It's as if everything moves but nothing moves, as if everything changes but nothing changes.

"So, when I move, I don't move and when I change, I don't change. I move but something within me doesn't move, and I change but something within me doesn't change—as if there's a stillness that stays the same no matter what I do.

"I don't know what this stillness is but it's undisturbed by whatever happens to me. Because it doesn't move, it doesn't change. Because it doesn't change, it stays the same. Because it stays the same, it's quiet and peaceful—like a balanced centre that's invisible and silent, always waiting to be discovered.

145

"It's as if this stillness is more than me, more than this person called Old Shu—as if it's something vast and timeless, something huge and immoveable, something that's both everywhere and nowhere.

"Although stillness is the name I give to it, I don't know what it is and I don't know when it came to be. Because I don't know where it is, I say it's within me—like a nameless place that's unaffected by everything I think and feel and do.

"So I honour this stillness as the very centre of myself, as the place where Old Shu and the Great Oneness are each other."

Strength

The Teaching:

When softness is strengthened with hardness and hardness is strengthened with softness, then hardness will be flexible, softness will be steadfast, and yielding will bend without breaking. When both softness and hardness are nurtured by discipline, then yielding has a resilience that survives the forces of adversity, and the endurance of strength is revealed. When both softness and hardness remember their place in wholeness, then yielding has a wisdom that surmounts the forces of adversity, and the endurance of strength prevails.

The Commentary:

"I watch the supple branches of willows bending in the storm's rage," said Old Shu, "and the tender strands of water-grasses swaying in the river's current. When their roots are set deeply, their outer form yields while their inner form holds. So I yield to the outer forces that I can't overcome and I rely on the inner strength that sustains me.

"By yielding to what I can't overcome, I become soft and compliant. By holding to what I honour, I become strong and enduring. By acknowledging both the inner and the outer, I choose a wisdom that follows the wordless way of the Great Oneness.

"Does this sound strange or impossible? The Great Oneness contains differences and contradictions. I'm small and insignificant but I'm also large and indestructible. The forces of the world move me at their whim yet I'm always myself, quiet and peaceful within the silence of my stillness. Because I'm always myself—because the outer can't overcome the inner—then the opposites live together in one balance.

"These opposites seem to be pulling against each other but they're really one force moving harmoniously together. When

147

I let the world have its way, it lets me have my way. When I accept it, it accepts me. We both change but we both stay the same. With this agreement, we move together as if we're each other.

"To move together like this, I must always remember the power of both the outer and the inner. If I don't yield to what's outside, my body will be killed. If I don't honour what's inside, my spirit will be killed. So I find a place in the middle where the inner and the outer can live together.

"This isn't so difficult to do—everyone who's still alive and who's still themselves has been doing it since they were born. But people complicate simple things by thinking too much. So I just do what I do, as if I'm doing nothing special. But I'm always aware of both the inner and the outer. And I always keep them together in my attention, as if I'm looking inward and outward at the same time.

"This is how I keep my balance amid everything's changing, how I find my simple place in the Great Oneness. And that's the only strength I need."

Suchness

The Teaching:

Without thinking, what is there to know? Without asking, what is there to answer? Without learning, what is there to forget? Without self, what is there to protect? Without a self, the centre of attention is everywhere. Without a word, the sound of silence speaks. Without an answer, the end of questions is reached. Without the clutter of explanations, the obvious is apparent. Then things are just themselves, and the brilliant clarity of suchness finds itself. Therefore, be silent and hear, forget and be free, release and be found, empty and be filled.

The Commentary:

"I walk. I talk. I see. I eat. I breathe," said Old Shu. "That's good enough for me. Why should anything be more complicated than that?

"When I hear, I just hear. When I sit, I just sit. Hearing explains hearing. Sitting explains sitting. What's the use of trying to explain something with something else? Then I'd have to explain the explaining and I'd never reach the end of explanations. The result would be such a tangle of words and thoughts that no one could be at ease with anything. And what would be the wisdom of that?

"When a thing is just what it is, why ruin it with thinking? Why try to understand it with something that's not itself? Why create confusion when there isn't any? So I stop asking foolish questions and I just let things be what they are.

"When I don't think about things — when I don't judge or compare — everything's uncomplicated. When I'm in balance with myself — when I've found my own stillness — I become selfless and thoughtless, clear and empty, open and receptive. By not considering what's inside, I don't disturb what's outside. With nothing to separate myself from everything else, awareness seems to arise from nowhere—within a place that doesn't seem to be me. Then I experience things exactly as they are. And so, with a wonderful simplicity and vivid clarity, each thing is just itself."

Teaching

The Teaching:

> *Those who have only answers will teach what is foolish and dangerous. Those who have only questions will teach what is temporary and insubstantial. But those who have found the formless will teach what is honoured and lasting. Since doubt is the softness of opening that receives and certainty is the hardness of denial that closes, open rather than close. Forget answers and teach without certainties. Nurture humility. Foster inner discipline. Cultivate readiness. Since the greatest knowledge lies beyond answers, challenge those who profess to have certainties and encourage those who are brave enough to doubt. Engender wonder. Reveal the depth of the mysterious. Then let time teach its own lessons and allow wisdom to discover itself.*

The Commentary:

"Teaching can't happen without learning," said Old Shu. "so I don't know if I teach anything or not. When I talk with people, I just say the things that arise from within me, the thoughts that come without a thought of what I know. I seem to speak without answers. And without answers, I never know what to say. So I just talk, turning my thoughts over and over for others to hear.

"When I open to the stillness within myself, I say things I don't expect to say. Because I'm open, I say what comes from my deepest centre. Because of stillness, I stay balanced. Because of balance, I stay connected to the present and I attend to where I am. Because I attend to where I am, I become one with the grace of each moment. And in the grace of each moment, I'm both full and empty.

"I know nothing, so my teaching is pure. I believe nothing, so my teaching is simple. I judge nothing, so my teaching is impartial. Because I'm not concerned about myself, I become one with those who are with me. Because I have no answers, I trust

151

what's deeper than words can explain.

"When I open to this trust, the world floods me with itself. Then I fill with wonder and I'm alive in a mystery that's greater than my thoughts can think. So I say what will empty me, what will release the fullness that overflows within me. Sometimes the stillness that's deep within me laughs and sometimes it weeps because the weightless joy and sorrow will not be silent. And sometimes the joy and sorrow mingle together, so I don't know whether the stillness inside me is laughing or weeping.

"If I teach anything to anyone, it's because I offer the fullness that's within me, and I honour the Great Oneness that arises through me. Sometimes people think I'm confusing and sometimes they think I'm strange. But I just do what I do and say what I say.

"But whatever I do or say, I never disrespect people by placing myself above them, by pretending I know more than they do. Since everyone is living and breathing the same mystery, what could I teach them, and what could I know that they don't know?

"Maybe that's why people talk to me as if they're talking to themselves. Maybe what they learn from me is what they already know. And so they teach themselves and find their own path in the Great Oneness."

Thinking

The Teaching:

Forget answers. Give up ideas. Become questions. Let thoughts wander. Thinking straight cannot follow the crooked path of the unknowable. Little thoughts cannot understand the great mystery that contains all thoughts. Therefore, think big and think crooked. Follow the long and wandering journey of little thoughts until they find their way back to the beginning of themselves. Then enter the empty circle of their journey. Be silent and amazed. And without one more thought, forget thinking. The stillness between thoughts will remember what thinking cannot think.

The Commentary:

"I think," said Old Shu. "But I also think about thinking. And because I think about thinking, I'm able to reach the end of thinking.

"What do I mean? I mean that, just like one word comes after another word, one thought comes after another thought, forever chasing themselves in a circle of their own making. When I know this by thinking about thinking, why would I be foolish enough to chase thoughts with even more thoughts? Why would I want to trap myself within the limits of my own thoughts? To find what's beyond thoughts, I have to quiet my thinking until I find the stillness between thoughts.

"So I use my thinking about thinking to undo thinking, until I don't have any thoughts about anything—until I have only nameless urges that seem to rise through my feet, fill my bones, and guide me with thoughtless wisdom.

"What do I think about thinking? I don't trust it. And what do I think about thoughts? I don't take them seriously.

"The feet of people stand on Earth and their bodies grow

straight and tall toward Heaven. When they're young, their hearts are open, their heads are close to the ground and their thoughts are sensible. But the older and taller people get, the stranger their ideas become until their heads fill with nonsense.

"Here's a stick, say Emperor Yao's philosophers—this is sensible enough. Now, they say, break this stick in half today. Then break a half of the stick in half tomorrow. Then break a half of that half in half on the next day. How many times, they ask, can such a half be broken in half? These thinkers, with their heads in Heaven, say that in ten thousand generations there will still be a half to break in half. But who's going to find a stick that's just a speck of dust in a dusty ivory box? What if the dust escapes in a gust of wind? And who's going to recognize this dust from all the other dust, and break it in half again? Give me a whole stick or give me the dust of the dust, but don't trouble me with Heaven's fancy thinking.

"Because my body is bent double, my head is close to my feet and my eyes are pointed to the ground. So I stay connected to the soil and Earth of my beginning. My attention isn't distracted by somewhere else. When I walk, I just walk. When I stand, I just stand. Where I am is just where I am. And what I feel is just what I feel. Because my thinking and my feeling are each other, my head and my feet are always in agreement.

"When my head and my feet are in agreement, I'm undivided and whole. When I'm undivided and whole, I'm without questions or answers. Then, without thinking one thought, everything is clear."

Trust

The Teaching:

Birth trusts the wisdom of beginning, death trusts the wisdom of ending, and the same trust pervades every beginning and ending between birth and death. Without this trust, no one could find balance and stillness amid everything's moving and changing. Without this balance and stillness, no one could ever find contentment and peace. Beyond the little shadows of self and doubt, everything moves within the wisdom of its changing, and so the quiet of trust accepts the arrival of each unfolding moment.

The Commentary:

"Flowing water doesn't know where to find the sea," said Old Shu, "but it follows a downward course and always arrives where it belongs. Why should it be any different for me? Trust is all I have. So each moment, I trust my body to take another breath and my heart to take another beat. At night when I fall asleep, I trust I'll awake in the morning. I trust my eyes to see and my ears to hear. I trust my feet to carry me across fields and along mountain paths. I trust my belly to announce that it's hungry and my bones to declare that their tired. I trust the honesty of my deepest feelings and I trust the wordless urges that guide me from moment to moment.

"Why do I trust? Because there's nothing else I can do. I have to trust. If I can't trust anything, then I can't even trust my own distrust. So trust is the only choice I have.

"Without trust, I'd be forever at war with the Great Oneness. Everything would be an enemy. My inner peace would become an uneasy victory, my wonder would turn into fear, my freedom would be a prison of endless struggle. I couldn't even trust tomorrow's sun to rise or the warmth of spring to follow the cold of winter. Trust is the acceptance that each new moment asks of me, the choice I must happily make if I'm to welcome — rather than dread — whatever comes.

155

"So I trust the wisdom that holds me in the wholeness of each moment. Because I accept what is, I ask for nothing and I desire nothing. Why would I change anything for anything else and ask for something that the Great Oneness hasn't already provided?"

Uselessness

The Teaching:

Success will never fulfil ambition. Possessions will never satisfy greed. Indulgence will never diminish desire. Victory will never appease power. Effort will never attain perfection. Those with wealth will be measured by their riches. Those with power will be judged by their influence. Those with loyalty will be known by their service. Those with bravery will be honoured by their deeds. Those with ability will be recognized by their usefulness. So become useless. Abandon the pursuit of wealth and power. Give up ambition and success. Forget fancy ideas and perfection. Stop meddling in the affairs of others. Do not try to change the way things are. Let things change themselves. Follow the course that has no name. Nurture simplicity. Disappear into the ordinary. Welcome the unknowable and accept its wisdom. Serve only the formless and be free from the burden of struggle. When uselessness has been mastered, the usefulness that is necessary will make itself known.

The Commentary:

"My body is bent with deformity," said Old Shu, "and my skin is wrinkled and weathered. I'm unfit for work or war and I'm too unsightly for dignified gatherings or elegant courts. Like the gnarled and knotted wood of an old tree, I'm useless, good for nothing. Because no one can find a use for me, they leave me alone to be who I am. So I just go on my peaceful way without disturbing the natural order of things.

"Trouble is caused by people who try to be useful. With their big ideas and fancy plans they think they know how things should be. So they employ the efforts of useful people to fix what they think needs fixing. And what's the result? Just more trouble. When they're finished changing things, the problems are bigger and more complicated than before. What was once a minor difficulty is now a major disaster, and a little inconvenience that would have solved itself is now an impossible mess.

"As for me, I don't have any plans and I have no idea of how things should be. I just do as little as possible. That's how I serve the will of nature and how I don't disturb the accord that guides the becoming and passing of all things. Because I don't try to change what's coming and I don't hold on to what's passing, I don't interfere with the unfolding order. Thus I move in harmony with the wisdom of the Great Oneness.

"Because I'm useless, I'm not used by the grand pursuits of noble people in high places. Because I look strange, I'm not taken seriously by those seeking influence and reputation. Because I'm unimportant, I'm not a threat to those with ambition. And people who want power leave me in peace because they think I'm of no use to them."

Walking

The Teaching:

Weight shifts in the unfolding demand of the present, and trust moves to its necessary place in the next step. In an easy spontaneity of unbroken movement, one step follows another. As each separate step becomes the next, all the different parts of walking disappear and its undivided flow becomes apparent. Without parts, where is left or right? Where is up or down? Where is here or there? Separateness disappears. Doubt is gone. Even balance is forgotten as movement becomes only itself. And then, in the simple elegance of ordinary walking, the essence of wholeness is glimpsed.

The Commentary:

"When I walk," said Old Shu, "I walk peacefully, at ease with the ground beneath my feet. I trust the wisdom that supports the small weight of my brief passing. And because I accept the mountains and the valleys as equals in the Great Oneness, uphill and downhill are the same to me. So, step after step, I seem to move without moving, as if walking is a living stillness that's neither inside nor outside of me.

"Although my body is bent and crooked, my legs are straight and nimble, loose and free. With a mind of their own, they move quickly and confidently, effortlessly following the contours of wherever they go. On the level paths of the Wu Valley, I glide as easily as if I'm floating on water. On the steep slopes of Mount Shan, my movements are fluid and certain, spontaneous and sure — like a stream laughing its way down to the Han River. As a wonder beyond wonder, my legs always keep my feet beneath me. When I trust their walking, I'm never tripped by stones or fooled by slippery places.

"When I walk, I walk with my feet and I let go of everything else. I trust their judgment and I let each foot follow the other in the flowing rhythm of their steps. I let them find their own way. And with a mind of their own — wherever they go — they know what to do.

"So my feet do the walking for me. And because I don't interfere, I walk without walking. That's why my feet are always ready for whatever happens, always prepared for whatever each step may bring.

"When I walk without walking, I move gracefully in the fullness of wherever I am. With my body embraced by the sky and my feet welcomed by the ground, I'm connected to both Heaven and Earth. Then crows will sometimes perch on my neckbone for smooth and lazy rides from one field to another. Sometimes their visits are noisy. But mostly they just ride quietly, at ease with my easiness."

Wandering

The Teaching:

The way is winding and crooked, surprising and ever-changing, forever unpredictable yet unerring. Therefore, soften and yield, bend and be flexible. Follow a wayward wisdom and trust a course that wanders. Honour the urges that arise from deep within the selfless centre of awareness—honour them but keep them distantly present and free like things formless and intangible. Discover directions without directions. Be patient and calm while waiting for openings. Then let the finding find itself.

The Commentary:

"I follow a crooked path that takes me where it will," said Old Shu. "So I never know where I'm going and I'm always lost. Sometimes the path bends to the right and sometimes to the left. Sometimes it goes up or down and sometimes here or there. Sometimes it seems to go in circles. But I just follow, wherever it goes.

"Sometimes the rocks are jagged and treacherous. Sometimes the slopes are steep and slippery. I encounter the unexpected around sharp bends. But I just keep wandering in an aimless way, meeting whatever I meet with calm acceptance.

"All my senses fill with the delights of everything that happens. Sights and sounds enchant me. Even though I don't know where I am or where I'm going, I feel contented and peaceful, full of the richness that each moment offers.

"Does anyone else know where they're going? Does anyone else know what will happen next? Am I the only one who's lost and wandering on this crooked path between birth and death?

"Sometimes I try to go straight but I meet obstacles I can't overcome. Sometimes I try to understand where I'm going but I can't find answers that make sense.

"So I just go where I go, meeting what I meet and becoming what I become. I rest when I'm tired and I eat when I'm hungry. Each step brings surprises and wonder. But I just wander on, enchanted and amazed by everything that happens.

"Sometimes this crooked path seems to have a direction that I almost remember, as if it's taking me somewhere I've been before. I encounter new things and new places but they seem distantly familiar, as if they're where they belong—as if the surprises aren't quite surprises and my amazement is about something else.

"Maybe I'm just where I'm supposed to be, just following my own path, somehow becoming myself. And maybe that's how I find my rightful place in the order of things. So maybe I'm not really wandering at all."

Wholeness

The Teaching:

Because of wholeness, all the imagined parts of differences appear and disappear yet everything is in balance with everything else. Enter the stillness of this balance to find wholeness. Although wholeness cannot be divided, it has parts. Although it is forever the same, it is forever changing. So move without moving and change without changing. Embrace contradictions. Discover the place between opposites where differences are themselves yet are more than themselves. Be larger than confusion. Become more than differences. Beyond all the differences invented by thoughts, a silent knowing remembers an undisturbed wholeness that has no name. Therefore, return to the beginning before beginnings, to the wholeness that is simply itself.

The Commentary:

"Because my chin rests on my bellybutton," said Old Shu, "my head and my body are close together. Before my head can get lost in some foolish idea, my belly has a talk with it and they come to an agreement. So I think what I feel and I feel what I think. And the two separate parts of myself become one wholeness.

"Most people get confused because their body parts are too far away from each other. With their feet on the ground and their heads in the sky, they feel one thing but they think another. The wisdom of Earth arises from below, the ideas of Heaven descend from above, and the two collide in the middle in a tangle of disagreement.

"Now look at me. I'm bent so double and my head's so close to the ground, my thoughts can't escape the wisdom of Earth and the ideas of Heaven have no place to enter.

"Maybe that's why I've never been able to understand a

163

Heaven that's separate from Earth. Whenever I try to think high and lofty thoughts, my nose smells the urgings of the soil and my head remembers where it's pointed. Then the ground pulls me back where I belong and Heaven disappears like a forgotten dream. So, wherever I am, my thoughts and my feelings are bound together like the parts of one living wholeness."

Woman

The Teaching:

The womb of darkness opens and birth arrives. The womb of light closes and death arrives. So woman is the living mystery of life and death embodied in flesh. She is the sadness in smiles, the sorrow in joy, the tears in laughter, the shadowed lining of loss that is hidden at the edge of each and every blessing. She is the round fullness of soft knowing, the waiting patience of slow time, the stillness in all changing, the only answer to the one single question that is more ancient than thoughts can think. Within the dark moving of her secret flesh is the moist beginning of breath and heartbeat. So she is urge and desire, invitation and fulfilment—and the eventual undoing of all doing. Therefore, to know woman beyond a simple knowing, summon a bravery that is deeper than the breath she gives, a resolve that is stronger than the death she promises. Risk everything. Abandon hope. Forget despair. Leave questions and doubts behind. For wordless answers, pass beyond the gates of reason and self. Yield to mystery's calling. Enter the light of woman's darkness and become the soft knowing of acceptance.

The Commentary:

"I'm not a woman," said Old Shu, "so there are things I can't know about women. And I can't talk about women as a woman because I'm a man. But, as a man, I know something about women that not even women know. And I have some woman in me that I can know, so maybe I can say something about women that will say something about men, too.

"As a man, I try to perfect the things that make me a man, and then I cultivate the woman in myself. Why? So I can be a man but I can also be more than a man. With the woman in myself, I can find the softness and the acceptance that reaches a deeper kind of understanding. By thinking less and feeling more, I can open and receive the wisdom of the world—and I can welcome the fullness of wonder.

165

"I look and I see how the emptiness of sky encloses the highest mountains, how the stillness of valleys accepts the greatest rivers, how the darkness of night holds the treasures of the day. With the woman in myself, I can meet my own darkness and become one with the mystery of all that holds me.

"To know the mystery that holds me, I enter the depth of my own darkness. I reach beyond answers to learn what answers cannot teach. I ask beyond questions to find what questions cannot ask. How can I do these things if I don't become more than a man?

"Although I search, a stillness within me stays serene and unmoved. Although I find, a darkness within me reaches beyond understanding. When I search, I move in this stillness. And when I find, I know with this darkness. Because the stillness in this dark mystery is the birth of my beginning and the source of my death, how can I not acknowledge the woman in myself?

"Women know of this dark mystery because they're the living body of it. But I'm a man, a hard and passing thing of restless thought and searching light who seeks to find the softness that women already know.

"So I soften and the softness of the world strengthens me. I wonder and the wonder of the world enlivens me. I empty and the emptiness of the world encloses me. When I'm accepted in the embrace of emptiness, the mystery of the world informs me. When I cultivate stillness, the stillness of the world moves me. When I welcome darkness, the darkness of the world comforts me. When I'm quiet in the comfort of darkness, I recognize the woman that's everywhere. And so I honour the other part of my own wholeness."

Words

The Teaching:

What can words say about things that are not words? What can sounds say about silence? Where is the silence between words that says what cannot be said? Who can use silence to say more than silence? Who can use words to say more than words? Between words is the silent word that cannot be said. Between thoughts is the formless thought that cannot be thought. Since the greatest thoughts are formless and the greatest words are silent, then deep-listen to hear what cannot be heard.

The Commentary:

"I use words," said Old Shu, "but I don't trust them. How can words that are just themselves say something about something that's not words? So I use words very carefully.

"When each thing is just what it is, why shape it in the form of a word by giving it a name? How can something be its name? Naming just conceals what things are and causes confusion. A stone doesn't call itself a stone. A fish doesn't call itself a fish. The wind is the sound of itself. A mountain shouts its own silence. By finding what has no words, I've learned the meaning of words.

"Words are very clever—too clever to be used carelessly. They name things that no one can find and they ask questions that no one can answer. They think their own thoughts, reach their own conclusions, pronounce their own truths, and carry on as if they had a mind of their own. If people could only hear what their words were saying, they wouldn't talk so much.

"So I use words to say what words can't say. I see without words. I hear without words. Then I listen to the fullness of everything I can't say. And when I'm free of words, I think without words and I understand without words. Why should my thoughts be confined to what words can say?

"At first, when I was very young, I had no words. I didn't know about names or understanding, about knowing or not knowing. Yet my eyes were open wide, I saw what I saw and I filled with the simple clarity of thoughtless seeing. Then I learned words. And the more I talked, the less I saw. Finally, I became so enchanted with words and all their thoughts that I talked even more, said even less, and saw nothing at all.

"Now that I've learned the meaning of words, I can see again. I talk but the things I say aren't really important. I use words but I'm always listening to what I can't say.

"When I listen to what I can't say, I hear my words saying less and less until they sound silly and useless. Without the burden of their meaning, I'm released into some place that's wordless and boundless. Then my thoughts become still, my awareness deepens, my eyes well with tears, and I'm overcome by a silence that fills me to overflowing.

"How can I explain this most profound silence? How can I explain the wonderful fullness that fills me to overflowing? How can I explain that I'm peacefully confused, contentedly bewildered, serenely lost in a nameless mystery that's too amazing for words?"

The Epilogue

In the months and seasons following Sung-chi's agreement with Old Shu, the two met as frequently as opportunity allowed. Sometimes Mei-lin was able to join them. As planned, Sung-chi brought a copy of the manuscript from the mysterious sage of Mount Shan. And, as intended, it became the beginning of Old Shu's teaching of Sung-chi.

During the second winter, sparks from an unattended cooking fire ignited the Kai-tung Monastery, destroying it and all its contents. The monks, now homeless, were taken in by the villagers of Ch'ang-an and the farmers of the Wu Valley. In gratitude, many of these monks helped in the homes, shops and farms where they were lodged. When spring came, some monks left for other monasteries but most went back to the razed site to begin rebuilding. Only one monk did not return to monastic life. He remained with his host family, a local vegetable farmer.

The riddle of the strange manuscript found by the Tien-po Temple was never solved, although interest waned after it had burned in the Kai-tung fire. And the villagers of Ch'ang-an never found the mysterious sage of Mount Shan, nor did they ever climb the mountain in search of him.

For many years, Old Shu continued to wander the paths of the Wu Valley, disappearing and then reappearing as he was inclined to do. In later years, some people thought he spent more of his time at a farm where a young family lived. But no one knew for certain because they paid little attention to the affairs of a strange, old hunchback.

Printed in the United States
by Baker & Taylor Publisher Services